Mediating Power-Sharing

T0373696

This book focuses on the design and operation of power-sharing in deeply divided societies. Beyond this starting point, it seeks to examine the different ways in which consociational institutions emerge from negotiations and peace settlements across three counter-intuitive cases – post-Brexit referendum Northern Ireland, the Brussels Capital Region and Cyprus. Across each of the chapters, the analysis assesses how the design or mediation of these various forms of power-sharing demonstrate similarity, difference and complexity in how consociationalism has been conceived of and operated within each of these contexts. Finally, a key objective of the book is to explore and evaluate how ideas surrounding power-sharing have evolved and changed incrementally within each of the empirical contexts. The unifying argument in the book is that power-sharing has to have the capacity to adapt to changing political circumstances, and that this can be achieved through the interplay of formal and informal micro-level refinements to these institutions and the procedures that govern them, which allow such institutions to evolve over time in ways that increase their utility as conflict transformation governance structures for deeply divided societies.

This book fills the gap in the published literature between theoretical and empirical studies of power-sharing, and will be of much interest to students of peace and conflict studies, consociationalism, European politics and IR in general.

Feargal Cochrane is Professor of International Conflict Analysis and the Director of the Conflict Analysis Research Centre (CARC), University of Kent, UK. He is author of nine books, including *Northern Ireland: The Reluctant Peace* (2013).

Neophytos Loizides is Professor in International Conflict Analysis, University of Kent, UK, and author of *Designing Peace: Cyprus and Institutional Innovations in Divided Societies* (2016).

Thibaud Bodson is a PhD candidate in the Human Rights Under Pressure Joint Interdisciplinary Doctoral Program at the Freie Universität Berlin, Germany, and Hebrew University of Jerusalem, Israel.

Mediating Power-Sharing

Devolution and Consociationalism in
Deeply Divided Societies

**Feargal Cochrane, Neophytos Loizides
and Thibaud Bodson**

LONDON AND NEW YORK

First published 2018
by Routledge

2 Park Square, Milton Park, Abingdon, Oxfordshire OX14 4RN
52 Vanderbilt Avenue, New York, NY 10017

Routledge is an imprint of the Taylor & Francis Group, an informa business

First issued in paperback 2020

British Library Cataloguing-in-Publication Data
A catalogue record for this book is available from the British Library

Library of Congress Cataloging-in-Publication Data
Names: Cochrane, Feargal, author. | Loizides, Neophytos,
    1974– author. | Bodson, Thibaud, author.
Title: Mediating power-sharing: devolution and consociationalism
    in deeply divided societies / Feargal Cochrane, Neophytos
    Loizides and Thibaud Bodson.
Description: New York : Routledge, [2018] | Includes
    bibliographical references and index.
Identifiers: LCCN 2017049649 | ISBN 9780815370178 (hardback) |
    ISBN 9781351250566 (ebook)
Subjects: LCSH: Peace-building—Case studies. | Institution
    building—Case studies. | Conflict management—Political
    aspects—Case studies. | Polarization (Social sciences)—Case
    studies. | Northern Ireland—Politics and government—1998– |
    Râegion de Bruxelles-Capitale (Belgium)—Politics and
    government. | Cyprus—Politics and government—2004–
Classification: LCC JZ5538 .C64 2018 | DDC 303.6/9—dc23
LC record available at https://lccn.loc.gov/2017049649

ISBN: 978-0-8153-7017-8 (hbk)
ISBN: 978-0-367-60724-1 (pbk)

Typeset in Times New Roman
by Apex CoVantage, LLC

Contents

Figures and tables

Figures

Tables

Acknowledgements

The themes and arguments at the centre of this book have been developed over the past three years in a range of settings at the University of Kent and beyond at academic conferences, workshops at Kent and in Ankara, Belfast and Nicosia, as well as through our other research and teaching activities.

We owe a debt of gratitude to a number of friends and colleagues (academic and policy practitioners) for their own contributions on the debates at the centre of this book, which we have benefitted from and incorporated into our own thinking on the operation of power-sharing in deeply divided societies. Feargal and Neophytos would particularly like to thank our colleagues in the School of Politics and International Relations and the Conflict Analysis Research Centre (CARC) at the University of Kent, for providing us with an intellectually supportive environment within which to work. Thibaud is grateful to Hans Kremer from the BCR delegation to Berlin for his clarifications on the 2017 political crisis between French-speaking political parties in Belgium. Many thanks also to Michael Giesen for his critical insights and to Dave Braneck for his help in editing Chapter 2. Research for Chapter 3 was supported by the ESRC and the Leverhulme Trust, for which Neophytos would also like to thank Iosif Kovras, Charis Psaltis and Djordje Stefanovic.

A particular note of thanks is due to the financial support provided by the School and Faculty of Social Sciences at Kent for a number of workshops where we have teased out some of the themes and arguments discussed in the book. One of these took place in Belfast on 24 June 2016 (the day after the UK referendum on EU membership) and we would like to thank the participants for sticking with the agenda, given the tumultuous political events of that morning. We would like to thank Northern Ireland's leading public affairs company, Stratagem International, and its director (and CARC Senior Research Fellow) Quintin Oliver and Conor Daly, for all of the work they put into that event as our local organising partner. These events and the numerous discussions before, during and after them, provided us with invaluable insights and ideas related to the comparative dimensions of power-sharing and its applicability across contexts. We would like to thank the participants at those workshops for their expertise and perspectives on the capacities and limitations of power-sharing across a range of regional cases, including: Professor Rupak Chattopadhyay, Yeshim Harris, Professor Cathy Gormley-Heenan, Professor Landon Hancock, Judith Large, Alan Leonard, Alan Meban, Professor John McGarry, Seamus McAleavy, Alban McGuinness, John McCallister, Professor Stevo Pendarovski, Dr Alex Schwartz, Dawn Purvis, Anthony Soares, and Alan Whysall.

Finally, we would like to thank two anonymous reviewers for their helpful comments on the proposal and to Andrew Humphrys, Hannah Ferguson and the team at Routledge for their advice and guidance at various stages of the project.

The usual health warnings apply: all errors of fact and interpretation remain entirely our own.

Abbreviations

BBF	Bizonal, Bicommunal Federation
BCR	Brussels Capital Region
CCC	Common Community Commission
CTA	Common Travel Area
DSG	Dutch-speaking Group (within the BCR parliament)
DUP	Democratic Unionist Party
FCC	Flemish Community Commission
FsCC	French-speaking Community Commission
FSG	French-speaking Group (within the BCR parliament)
GC	Greek Cypriots
GFA	Good Friday Agreement
IICIR	Intergovernmental and Inter-parliamentary Conference for Institutional Renewal
MLA	Member of the Legislative Assembly
NI	Northern Ireland
OFMDFM	Office of First Minister and Deputy First Minister
PfG	Programme for Government
SDLP	Social Democratic and Labour Party
SF	Sinn Fein
SHA	Stormont House Agreement
TC	Turkish Cypriots
UN	United Nations
UUP	Ulster Unionist Party

Introduction

The idea of sharing power in deeply divided societies as a means of increasing the incentives for co-operation between political adversaries is not a new one. The study of consociationalism has also been a mainstay of academic debates in political science for some time. Classical consociational theory was popularised (though not invented) by Arend Lijphart (1968, 1969) and was subsequently developed by other scholars (Steiner, 1971; Nordlinger, 1972).[1] More recent interventions have sought to add various refinements to Lijphart's model and address criticisms regarding its conceptual clarity and operational dexterity (Loizides, 2016; O'Leary, 1989; McGarry & O'Leary, 1995, 2004, 2006). Consociationalism and power-sharing are not synonymous terms, but they are related and overlapping approaches designed to engineer political accommodation in deeply divided societies.

Power-sharing might appear to be a common sense approach to conflicts that have ended, or been suspended, without a clear outcome. It avoids the 'winners and losers' result in contexts where there are no clear victors or vanquished – and provides those who have the capacity to keep violent conflict going with an alternative political route. While power-sharing is unlikely to fulfil the full aims and objectives of the conflict parties, it has the capacity to provide sufficient gains and adequate safeguards to allow groups to move out of violence and into new political structures. Varieties of consociational power-sharing also tend to be popular among conflict parties themselves, which in part explains why settlements driven by internal negotiations and consensus-based agreements tend to exhibit such features (Bieber, 2013). Indeed, the consociational model, which recognises ethnonational group rights and provides mutual vetoes within the political structures, tends 'to be demanded by conflict parties that fear being outvoted, either now or in the future' (Caspersen, 2017, 70). In this sense, it is the logical institutional outcome that conflict parties can sign up to when they do not trust other partners in government and where numerous goals and grievances at the heart of the conflict remain either unresolved or unclear.

This could be viewed as a pessimistic starting point for efforts to build stable political institutions in deeply divided societies – and it has been by many scholars, as detailed below. However, we do not take this view and believe that with the correct set of conditions that allow power-sharing systems to adapt, evolve and incorporate dispute mechanisms that respond to their local context, they represent the most viable approach to political institution building available to deeply divided societies riven by ethnonational or ethnolinguistic cleavages.

While sharing power may seem like a reasonable approach to those outside such conflicts, it is far from being an uncontentious option and working out how best to design power-sharing political systems has been a central debate in political science, comparative politics and peace and conflict studies for at least a generation. As indicated in the following chapter on Northern Ireland, in societies where an insecure majority lives uneasily with a large minority, the first instinct of the former may not be to share power with the latter. This was summed up by Horowitz's (2002) observation that a majority conflict party will be reluctant to share power if they can govern on their own. As the next chapter indicates, this was very much the case in the context of Northern Ireland from its founding in 1921 until the majoritarian parliament was suspended by the British government in 1972. It took another generation before unionists accepted that a majoritarian system of government was not likely to be viable and that power-sharing with the nationalist/republican community was required for devolved government to be restored. The motivation for majorities to share power with minorities is generated through incentives (positive and negative) that emerge across different contexts. These might include international pressure, recognition of a 'looming catastrophe'/worsening of violent conflict, or fear of long-term erosion of a majority position (Caspersen, 2017, 71). Expressed more positively, such incentives could involve the opening up of new financial opportunities or access to new political and economic relationships.

There has been an energetic scholarly and policy debate surrounding the suitability of power-sharing in the pursuit of political stability in deeply divided societies. At a more operational level, there has been a detailed discussion around different models of power-sharing systems designed to provide incentives for political co-operation in ethnically divided societies. The literature on consociationalism and its alternatives has highlighted a set of unresolved tensions between its advocates and critical admirers on the one hand (Lijphart, 2004; McCrudden, McGarry, O'Leary & Schwartz, 2016; McGarry & Loizides, 2015) and its scholarly opponents on the other, who advocate a more integrationist or 'centripetal' approach as an alternative to consociational power-sharing (Barry, 1975; Dixon, 2002; Horowitz, 1991, 1993, & 2002; Lustick, 1997; Reilly, 2012; Taylor, 2009).

The centripetal approach popularised by Horowitz (1991), seeks to provide incentives to break down ethnonational barriers rather than acknowledge and accommodate them within the political structures. At the heart of the various suggestions from this approach for building new political institutions lies a desire to develop political incentives that will integrate, rather than accommodate, rival ethnonational projects in deeply divided societies. Centripetal institutions and electoral systems are designed to promote positive incentives for inter-ethnic co-operation and encourage political moderation, rather than rewarding what are regarded as the centrifugal forces of ethnic outbidding and rigid ethnocentrism, often seen at elections in deeply divided societies. As Reilly states, centripetal strategies are designed to encourage 'politicians to do more than just shop for votes in their own community' (Reilly, 2002) and to provide incentives to the electorate to look around for alternatives before casting their vote. Critics of the integrationist model see it as providing insufficient guarantees of protection for minorities within the political institutions and inadequate evidence that the built-in incentives for moderation and integration would work in practice. While integrationists frame consociational accommodationists as being overly pessimistic about the capacity of deeply divided societies to transcend their ethnocentrism, the proponents of consociationalism can, for their part, point to the lack of verifiable evidence to support the integrationist position. At best a benign majoritarianism, based on a patron/client relationship between the majority and minority; at worst, the freezing out of the minority from effective citizenship and the creation of monopoly control for the majority community.

Mediating Power-Sharing draws on both of these perspectives but is aligned more clearly to the former, and seeks to make a theoretical and empirical contribution surrounding the capacity of power-sharing to assist the process of conflict transformation in deeply divided societies. This book supports the desirability of power-sharing institutions in deeply divided societies while recognising their rigidity in practice, particularly in the process of mediating and renegotiating key provisions over time. (See Bodson & Loizides 2017; Cochrane, 2012, 2013; Loizides, 2016.)

Our aim in the three chapters of the book is to contribute to understandings of how power-sharing is mediated within deeply divided societies and the ways in which consociational institutions may adapt more nimbly to changing political contexts. The book seeks to provide a new framework for consociational power-sharing, establishing a bridge between the accommodationist and integrationist models of institutional design. The cases of Brussels, Northern Ireland and Cyprus fit into a continuum in terms of peace settlement indicators. In terms of this book's case selection, their very different characteristics, in terms of history, geography and peace settlement context, provide us with the confidence that findings are likely to be generalizable to other similarly divided societies.

The following chapter, which focuses on Northern Ireland, charts the challenges that have faced and continue to face power-sharing, but also recognises that devolution has become by far the most popular political alternative in the region, despite its problematic implementation. Figures from the 2016 *Northern Ireland Life and Times Survey* indicate that there is a general consensus in Northern Ireland for the region to remain part of the UK with its own devolved government. This secured 54% support, far outweighing the main alternatives offered, remaining part of the UK with direct rule (12%) or to reunify with the rest of Ireland (19%).[2] This chapter examines how power-sharing evolved across different phases from outright rejection by unionists in the 1970s, to partial acceptance by the 1990s, into more comprehensive endorsement since 2007. It also demonstrates the dysfunctional aspects of power-sharing in Northern Ireland that have led to endemic instability and poor levels of governance in the region.

Chapter 1 highlights how the interplay of formal and informal institutional reforms have produced an iterative and fluid system of power-sharing in Northern Ireland. It also demonstrates the importance of exogenous changes and how these can affect the endogenous dynamics of power-sharing institutions. The UK referendum on EU membership in June 2016, and the period of negotiation that has followed, has had a significant external impact on devolved government in Northern Ireland and provides an example of how institutions can be influenced by unforeseen changes in the external political context.

This first chapter provides some evidence to suggest that consociationalism does not need to be a closed or static system of political accommodation, but can evolve and mutate as a result of formal and informal revisions towards a more integrative space, as envisioned by the proponents of centripetalism. We suggest here that it is feasible to both envisage and engineer a form of consociational power-sharing that retains adequate protections for ethnic minorities, while also developing integrative incentives over time. These were embryonic in the Northern Ireland context, but were significant nonetheless, and served as an indicator that zero-sum ethnonational equations, where success for one was seen as defeat for the other, could be replaced by positive-sum outcomes, where interests are regarded as being interdependent rather than distinct. The power-sharing institutions that were established in Northern Ireland helped to demonstrate the capacity for political accommodation to evolve over time into something that might be termed 'accommodation+' (by this we mean something that falls short of an ethnically blind society but has moved some way beyond distinct accommodationist tramlines). While power-sharing structures in Northern Ireland were rooted in the latter, they aspired to, and have achieved, more than that. This was personified by the political careers of former First Minister Rev. Ian Paisley and former Deputy First Minister Martin McGuinness – both now deceased. For the short time that they were in government together (2007–2008) they established a relationship where they saw their interests as being overlapping rather than distinct, and they worked together for the political and economic benefit of everyone in Northern Ireland. The integrative aspect was embodied in Paisley's comment to McGuinness at their first meeting in 2007: 'We don't need Englishmen to rule us. We can do that ourselves.' They did this effectively for 13 months while never losing their sense of political identity as committed British unionist and Irish republican respectively. While it is important not to overstate this relationship, it provides an embryonic example that a sense of joint purpose can be produced within consociational institutions that can allow them to evolve into an accommodation+ space.

We argue here that the capacity of political institutions to evolve and reform is critical for their survival, not least to provide sufficient flex to adapt to unforeseen circumstances at the point such institutions were established (e.g. post-Brexit Northern Ireland). Power-sharing needs to have the capacity to adapt to local political conditions in ways that allow it to take advantage of changing political contexts over time. Institutional systems that are needed at the beginning of a conflict transformation process may not be optimal several years afterwards, and the political fabric needs to have the capacity to stretch and adapt over time, to best reflect this changing context. Belgium and Brussels are two good examples of this principle. Belgium has gone through six revisions of its constitution since 1970 in order to reshape its institutions and to grant its community groups a certain degree of cultural and economic autonomy. With respect to the Belgian capital, the Brussels Capital Region (BCR) was created in 1989 as a constituent part of the Belgian federal structure. BCR institutions went through substantial modifications twice. The first time, it was at the fifth state reform, in 2001, and the second time at the sixth state reform, in 2011–12. At the time this book goes to press, discussions are ongoing about possible future reforms. Similarly, and as reflected in the chapter that follows on power-sharing in Northern Ireland, Mark Durkan, the former leader of the moderate nationalist Social Democratic and Labour Party (SDLP), reflected on the need for the institutions to evolve when speaking at the British Irish Association Conference at Oxford to mark the tenth anniversary of the Belfast/Good Friday Agreement (GFA). He commented specifically on the need to retain 'community designation' for those elected to the Northern Ireland Assembly in order to maintain proportionality in the power-sharing system between unionists and nationalists. Proportionality lies at the heart of the power-sharing system in Northern Ireland in order to ensure that there can be cross-community support for important decisions. To determine this proportionality it was necessary for those elected to the Northern Ireland Assembly to 'designate' themselves as being either a unionist or a nationalist – though it was also possible to opt out into an 'other' category. This was a rather crude but functional mechanism to allow for a system of cross-community votes and vetoes within the political institutions, but it was criticised by integrationists for building ethnonational divisions into the political system.

> I remember, at the time, saying that the system of designation was necessary because of what we were coming from but should not be necessary where we were going. I argued that such measures with their arguably sectarian or sectional undertones should be bio-degradable, dissolving in the future as the environment changed. Most, if not all of us, had such future adjustments in mind when we wrote the review mechanisms into the Agreement. As we move towards a fully sealed and settled process we should be preparing to think about how and when to remove some of the ugly scaffolding needed during the construction of the new edifice.[3]

Despite the mixed metaphor, this remains at best an aspiration rather than an achievement in the Northern Ireland context, as the consociational institutions are still dominated by fear of the past rather than hope for the future. While politics has evolved significantly since the GFA was reached in 1998, the political institutions have not adapted at the same pace.

The starting point for the three substantive chapters that follow is that power-sharing systems are the correct model for political reform of ethnonational conflicts – when properly understood, designed and operated. This does not underplay their inadequacies in practice, but it seeks to develop a new approach to the study of consociationalism that might provide enhanced ways of tackling weaknesses that have been identified in such institutional design.

Unlike critics of consociationalism, we argue that cross-community power-sharing/mutual vetoes and proportionality in government can all provide useful pillars in the system, underpinning confidence in at least the medium term. Equally, we argue that a static form of consociationalism without the capacity to change incrementally over time (to 'bio-degrade', as former SDLP leader Mark Durkan put it in 2008) is equally problematic.

This form of stasis can lead to inertia, dysfunction and complacency in government and to community disillusionment and apathy towards the political system more broadly.

Mediating Power-Sharing examines the different ways in which consociational institutions emerged from negotiations and peace settlements across three theoretically informative cases: Northern Ireland, the Brussels Capital Region and Cyprus. Across each of the chapters, we analyse how the design of these various approaches to power-sharing demonstrates similarity, difference and complexity in how consociationalism has been conceived and operated in each of these contexts. Thus, while proportionality is a key aspect of power-sharing in Northern Ireland, the book demonstrates how proportional representation of the French-speaking and the Dutch-speaking community groups in BCR was abandoned at the 2001 state reform. Proportional representation was then replaced by a system of guaranteed representation in which the Dutch-speaking minority would receive a fixed and over-proportional number of seats in the BCR parliament. The intention here is to demonstrate that there are multiple iterations of consociational power-sharing but that all of them are fluid, organic and evolving political systems. As such, they should be regarded as having the capacity to develop and change in conjunction with their political context, rather than being seen as fixed or static models of political accommodation in divided societies. The conclusion broadens this point further, by assessing how the three main cases discussed relate to possible institutional reform in other deeply divided societies, such as Bosnia, Syria or Sri Lanka.

Mediating Power-Sharing seeks to explore and evaluate how ideas surrounding consociational institutions have evolved incrementally within each of the empirical contexts. To date there has been a somewhat binary approach taken to accommodationist and integrationist models of power-sharing. The former seeks to contain and manage conflict between ethnonational adversaries, while the latter seeks to deconstruct and transform such divisions through institutions that reformulate existing ethnonational cleavages. In addition, the accommodationist approach has tended to focus on formal political institutions while the integrationist approach has generally favoured more incremental informal political change via non-statutory negotiation and through shared social space and cultural practice.

Mediating Power-Sharing suggests that there is potential for a symbiotic rather than adversarial relationship between these approaches. We argue that these are not binary opposites and can move into a new conceptual space that allows them to operate together in recognition of the fact that the political contexts they relate to are evolving rather than static. Each of the three chapters probes the potential for consociational power-sharing institutions to be combined with integrationist elements, particularly in the form of deadlock-resolving mechanisms to be used whenever power-sharing arrangements fail. The focus here is that greater attention needs to be paid to addressing problems in power-sharing systems in order that such societies are not limited to the management of conflict, but can occupy a space where the institutions promote positive incentives to overcome ethnonational divisions. This form of power-sharing is needed in order to move beyond institutional stability and non-violence towards a sense of joint enterprise and common purpose, where the society can move into a truly post-conflict environment.

The book focuses on an underexplored aspect of the power-sharing experience – namely the micro-level revisions and formal/informal processes that translate the theory of the institutions into their operational practice. The uniting argument in this book is that consociational power-sharing is an iterative rather than a closed system with relatively static mechanics. The chapters that follow demonstrate that power-sharing institutions need to have the capacity to adapt to changing political circumstances, and that this can be achieved through the interplay of formal and informal micro-level refinements to these institutions and the procedures that govern them.

In empirical terms, *Mediating Power-Sharing* provides a comparative analysis of three regions not previously examined together: Northern Ireland, Brussels Capital Region and Cyprus. These divided places provide an excellent comparison because they illustrate different stages of negotiation and institutional forms of power-sharing to deal with ethnonational divisions. They also span different timelines and levels of political conflict, from latent dynamics in Cyprus and BCR to manifest violence in Northern Ireland. They are also sufficiently overlapping as divided societies, despite their unique contexts, to provide for a useful comparison. Unlike BCR, both Cyprus and Northern Ireland are societies defined by two communities with 'conflicting self-determination aspirations' (McGarry, 2015, 265). They are both deeply divided societies that have in large degree been shaped by semi-external kin-states, Turkey and Greece in the case of Cyprus and Britain and the Republic of Ireland in the Northern Ireland context. But there are important and nuanced differences here. The kinship status is not the same and does not operate the same way in both places. Northern Ireland is not hanging between two patron states in the manner of Cyprus. It is constitutionally 'owned' in its territorial entirety by the UK, even if that is not unilaterally acknowledged in Northern Ireland. In addition, while a number of power-sharing initiatives have been attempted in Northern Ireland since the early 1970s and at the time of writing are still theoretically (if not actually) operational, Cyprus does not have a power-sharing structure, and has to look back to the 1960–1963 period for its own version of consociational government. Finally, while both are deeply divided societies with a binary ethnonational cleavage, Cyprus has experienced a latent or frozen conflict over the past 50 years, while Northern Ireland suffered direct violence for 30 years that has overtly affected the nature of the power-sharing institutions and the issues that they continue to face. The BCR and NI make a good comparison, because unlike Cyprus, they have both operated systems of power-sharing for a sustained period, and although they vary in their mechanics, they have both demonstrated the capacity to adapt to change over time. They also differ significantly, as the divisions in BCR are mainly over conflicting ethno-linguistic identities and, like Cyprus, conflict in BCR has mainly been latent rather than violent. The three chapters can thus be visualised as a three-part Venn diagram, with intersections between all three but large areas of unique context that needs to be reflected in the design of their power-sharing institutions.

Chapter 2 builds on the BCR case. BCR provides a unique system of regional and urban governance not widely researched in consociational studies. Power-sharing arrangements in Brussels have enabled the peaceful cohabitation of the two main ethnolinguistic groups, a French-speaking majority and a Dutch-speaking minority. Well-functioning and sustained power-sharing arrangements that provide the necessary flexibility to address changing political circumstances are relatively rare across deeply divided societies, which makes the BCR an intriguing comparison with the Northern Ireland case.

This chapter highlights how the contrasting political context in Brussels requires a significantly different model of power-sharing. This focuses on two critical features of broader interest to consociational theories, adaptability and co-operation. Firstly, the chapter discusses the establishment and the successive reforms of the BCR institutions. In that regard, it demonstrates how several legal procedures for institutional reforms exist in BCR which guarantee a certain flexibility for the institutions to adapt to changing political circumstances. Secondly, it presents some aspects of the current BCR institutions. In that respect, it shows how the BCR makes extensive use of institutional incentives for co-operation between community groups. In this chapter, we argue that the region's combination of flexible procedures for institutional reforms with an extensive set of co-decision mechanisms are key to guaranteeing adaptability and co-operation. A specific form of 'living consociationalism' is outlined here, where the political system has managed to mediate a number of different iterations without descending into the dysfunctional relationships outlined in the Northern Ireland case.

In this chapter, we show how BCR's adaptability is largely framed by the legal procedures at its disposal in order to undertake institutional reforms. In this framework, the Brussels model displays a set of three different procedures. The requirements and the degree of stringency of each procedure varies according to the nature and the importance of the demand raised by the community groups. In turn, institutional mechanisms requiring a high degree of co-operation between community groups in Brussels facilitate the use of this incremental set of reform procedures. An extensive list of institutional mechanisms has been designed for the protection of the Dutch-speaking minority in BCR. These mechanisms often provide for co-decision proceedings and thus for veto power for both community groups. The risks of institutional stalemates inherent to co-decision procedures have so far been largely avoided in BCR. This has resulted in a rather successful form of co-operation of both ethno-linguistic groups in Brussels and indeed a smooth co-administration of the Capital Region.

Another key issue highlighted in Chapter 2 relates to the treatment of proportional representation in BCR. The institutional adjustment mechanisms provided in the BCR power-sharing agreement were used to grant additional protection to the Dutch-speaking minority and led to a *de facto* transformation of proportional representation into a more sophisticated 'protective disproportional representation' model (Bodson & Loizides, 2017). This chapter assesses why and how the BCR model of power-sharing shifted in the 2001 Lombard agreement from the traditional proportional approach to one that enabled the *over-representation* of the Dutch-speaking minority. The chapter also charts the consequences of this reform and the degree to which over-representation can pose challenges for the promotion of justice, fairness and democracy. In the BCR, the over-representation of the Dutch-speaking group raises legal issues related to inter-group discrimination and to the right to equal representation. The abandonment of a system of proportional representation in BCR bucks the trend of perceived best practice in the literature on consociationalism, which typically stresses the importance of proportionality for the protection of minorities (Lijphart, 1968; McEvoy, 2013; McGarry & O'Leary, 2009). This is not without its own tensions and institutional limitations, but it does demonstrate the capacity of consociational power-sharing for conceptual and operational dexterity rather than a one-size-fits-all approach to political design in deeply divided societies.

The chapter also demonstrates that only 15 years after the adoption of a new representation model, additional reforms are being envisaged to adapt once again to the evolving political and sociological circumstances in Brussels. Arguments are still being raised for a correction of the 'protective disproportional representation' model, in favour of a more proportional system of representation. While significantly less dysfunctional than the current power-sharing experience in Northern Ireland, this chapter on the BCR demonstrates that disagreement remains over the correct balance between disproportional and proportional political systems in deeply divided societies.

Chapter 2 connects to the previous examination of power-sharing dynamics in Northern Ireland in another generic respect, namely the impact of unforeseen exogenous change on endogenous institutions. In the previous chapter this was framed in the context of the 2016 Brexit referendum and its ongoing impact on the political relationships in Northern Ireland and the viability of power-sharing in the region. In the BCR context, the exogenous dimension is provided by the impact of ethno-linguistic groups in other parts of Belgium, with their respective compatriots in Brussels. A breakdown in trust between the French-speaking Socialist Party and French-speaking Christian Democrat Party, over alleged corruption by the former, has infected the Brussels government where the Brussels members of both parties were co-operating. This seepage from beyond the BCR can act as a destabilizing factor on the subtle equilibrium of inter-group relations in Brussels and has placed a question mark over the continued operation of the current institutional arrangements. Overall, Chapter 2 provides an effective counterpoint to Chapter 1 on power-sharing in Northern Ireland by demonstrating that while the dynamics of the consociational systems are significantly different, both have experienced a degree of institutional evolution over time. While there are some points of overlap with power-sharing in Northern Ireland, Chapter 2 demonstrates how the design and operation of consociational institutions can differ.

Chapter 3 focuses on Cyprus and plays an interesting role in the context of the book in that Cyprus represents a deeply divided society that does not currently have a system of consociational power-sharing. In this respect it is in a position to avoid some of the scar tissue left by the Northern Ireland and BCR experiences and build on the lessons provided by other cases. Conversely, the chapter will demonstrate that unlike in Northern Ireland or BCR, neither of the ethnonational communities in Cyprus are as united on the fundamental architecture of power-sharing, or on the envisioned instruments of potential consociational institutions. This is in part because, unlike in the other two central cases explored in the book, power-sharing between Greek and Turkish Cypriots remains a struggle over rival projects of self-determination. (McGarry, 2015, 288). The catch-22 position in Cyprus is that the lack of functioning consociational institutions has impeded both sides from coming to an agreed position on the boundaries of their rival self-determination ambitions – yet achieving this is a necessary prerequisite for such institutions to be delivered. In Northern Ireland, on the other hand, the pain barrier on conflicting claims to national self-determination was mediated via political anaesthetic (referred to in much of the scholarly literature as 'constructive ambiguity') (Dixon, 2002; Tonge, 2014). The Belfast/Good Friday Agreement effectively parked the question of Northern Ireland's constitutional future and allowed the unionist and nationalist parties (and their supporters) to read it in different ways.

Cyprus mirrors Northern Ireland as the majority of political parties in both communities (and two motherlands) have endorsed a federal settlement since 1977 leaving little ambiguity as to the broader architecture of the future settlement. Although no final settlement has been reached since then, we argued that Cyprus has made important early steps in the past decade in terms of developing bi-communal projects and cooperation across a wide range of humanitarian, cultural, environmental, crisis management and other issues. This model of informal proto-consociational power-sharing could be particularly relevant for other 'frozen conflicts' around the world. We argue that Cyprus could also benefit from the conceptual innovations outlined across the Northern Ireland and Brussels Capital Region chapters. Yet, drawing on recent mediations, this chapter demonstrates the obstacles to establishing power-sharing institutions in deeply divided societies and the ways in which potentially viable reforms can be undermined by short-term political expediency.

Chapter 3 also explores the manner in which the concept of power-sharing has evolved in Cyprus over the past 40 years and how its specific political context will require an individually tailored form of consociationalism. A key focus of Chapter 3 is the relevance of the d'Hondt system (shared by Northern Ireland and discussed in Chapter 1) as a mechanism for providing a politically stable governing coalition. By incentivising the participation of all major parties in government, d'Hondt skips the problematic and time-consuming task of forming inter-ethnic governing coalitions. We argue that a d'Hondt system is highly relevant for Cyprus and that it could fit well with the specific character and needs of Cypriot political parties, replacing the cross-voting/presidential proposals as stipulated in the failed summer 2017 peace talks in Switzerland. At the same time, we recognise that the transfer of institutional designs from one political context to another is never an exact science and will produce its own specific challenges. The parallel of kinship states in the Cyprus and Northern Ireland contexts provides an example. There are ostensible similarities but significant differences on closer inspection. Unionists and nationalists in Northern Ireland have frequently looked to Britain and the Republic of Ireland respectively for some level of patron-state support in times of crisis, though this has always been somewhat fluid and inconsistent. More obviously, as Northern Ireland is wholly a devolved region within the UK, it can expect the national government to impose direct rule from London if power-sharing fails – a fail-safe, therefore, if things go badly wrong – and this may well be the likelihood during 2017 if inter-party talks between the DUP and Sinn Fein prove unable to restore the devolved institutions. Unsurprisingly, direct rule from Westminster was gradually introduced in Autumn 2017 so that a budget could be set for the region and public services could continue to function. However, a future reunited Cyprus cannot rely on similar arrangements involving Athens and Ankara that might be expected of Dublin and London. Neither Greece nor Turkey would be able to step in (or rather should be allowed to do so) as a third party to mediate disputes if power-sharing failed in a reunited Cyprus. To take account of this reality, Chapter 3 proposes a supplementary dimension to current consociational studies by reviewing alternative deadlock-breaking mechanisms if problems arise at different levels of governance in the cabinet, the parliaments, or any sub-unit of a future Cyprus federation.

We suggest that a semi-presidential system could be adopted in the Cyprus case, where two co-presidents would be elected through cross-community voting mechanisms, as was previously agreed by Cypriot leaders in 2009 and 2010. In common with the Northern Ireland model, executive power would still lie primarily with the cabinet. However, the two co-presidents would possess key arbitration powers to deal with an agreed list of critical issues, such as matters involving security and co-operation with the United Nations force on the island. However, the most important responsibility of the co-presidents would be to mediate and arbitrate deadlocks at all levels of government. The checks and balances suggested here aim to provide positive incentives for co-operation and stable government. They are based on an adaptation of consociationalism that builds on some of the lessons provided by the experience of power-sharing in Northern Ireland and the Brussels Capital Region.

The conclusion of the book aims to do two things. Firstly, it draws out some of the key similarities and differences in the three case studies of power-sharing at the heart of the book. These focus on the key interlocking themes that bind all three chapters together, notably the interplay of formal and informal adaptations in the political institutions; the capacity and need for power-sharing structures to evolve over time in line with the degree of available political space; and the relationship between changes in the exogenous political context and endogenous dynamics of the power-sharing institutions and the political parties that operate them. Secondly, the conclusion considers whether there are lessons from the case studies that may be applicable more broadly to other deeply divided societies, and how consociational theory might be further enhanced in these contexts.

Our objective, in the chapters that follow, is to make a contribution to consociational theory by illustrating the capacity of such institutions to evolve over time, to adapt and change in response to their different political contexts – and to provide the foundations for ethnonational groups to establish viable partnerships based on shared, rather than separate, goals. *Mediating Power-Sharing* is put forward as an opportunity to reflect on what consociational political institutions have struggled to accomplish and how they might work more effectively to build peace within deeply divided societies.

Notes

1   The key features of consociationalism have been traced back to the Netherlands in 1917 (McGarry and O'Leary, 1993).
2   www.ark.ac.uk/nilt/2016/Political_Attitudes/NIRELND2.html
3   Speech by Mark Durkan at British Irish Association Conference, Oxford, 5 September 2008. http://cain.ulster.ac.uk/issues/politics/docs/sdlp/md050908.htm

Bibliography

Barry, B. (1975) 'Political Accommodation and Consociational Democracy'. *British Journal of Political Science* 5 (4): 477–505.

Basta, K., McGarry, J., & Simeon, R. (2015) *Territorial Pluralism: Managing Differences in Multinational States*, UBC Press, Vancouver & Toronto.

Bieber, F. (2013) 'The Balkans: The Promotion of Power-Sharing by Outsiders' in McEvoy J. & O'Leary, B. (eds.) *Power-Sharing in Deeply Divided Places*, UPENN Press, Philadelphia, PA, pp. 312–326.

Bodson, T., & Loizides, N. (2017) 'Consociationalism in the Brussels Capital Region: Dis-Proportional Representation and the Accommodation of National Minorities' in McCulloch, A. & McGarry, J. (eds.) *Power-Sharing: Empirical and Normative Challenges*, Routledge, London.

Caspersen, N. (2017) *Peace Agreements*, Polity Press, Cambridge.

Cochrane, F. (2012) 'From Transition to Transformation in Ethnonational Conflict: Some Lessons from Northern Ireland.' *Ethnopolitics*, 11(2), 182–203.

Cochrane, F. (2013) *Northern Ireland: The Reluctant Peace*, London and New Haven: Yale University Press.

Dixon, P. (2002) 'Political Skills or Lying and Manipulation? The Choreography of the Northern Ireland Peace Process.' *Political Studies* 50 (3): 725–741.

Horowitz, D. (1991) *A Democratic South Africa? Constitutional Engineering in a Divided Society*, University of Calefornia Press, Berkeley.

Horowitz, D. (1993) 'The Challenge of Ethnic Conflict: Democracy in Divided Societies.' *Journal of Democracy* 4 (4): 18–38.

Horowitz, D. (2002) 'Explaining the Northern Ireland Agreement: The Sources of an Unlikely Constitutional Consensus.' *British Journal of Political Science* 32 (2): 193–220.

Lijphart, A. (1968) *The Politics of Accommodation: Pluralism and Democracy in the Netherlands*, University of Calefornia Press, Berkeley.

Lijphart, A. (1969) 'Consociational Democracy.' *World Politics*, 21 (2), 207–225.

Lijphart, A. (1977) *Democracy in Plural Societies: A Comparative Exploration*, New Haven: Yale University Press.

Lijphart, A. (2004) 'Constitutional Design for Divided Societies.' *Journal of Democracy* 15 (2), 96–109.

Loizides, N. (2016) *Designing Peace: Cyprus and Institutional Innovations in Divided Societies*, University of Pennsylvania Press, Pennsylvania.

Lustick, I. (1997) 'Lijphart, Lakatos, and consociationalism.' *World Politics* 50 (1): 88–117.

McCrudden, C., McGarry, J., O'Leary, B., & Schwartz, A. (2016) 'Why Northern Ireland's Institutions Need Stability.' *Government and Opposition* 51 (1): 30–58.

McEvoy, J. (2013) 'We Forbid! The Mutual Veto and Power-Sharing Democracy' in McEvoy, J. & O'Leary, B. (eds), *Power Sharing in Deeply Divided Places*, University of Pennsylvania Press, Philadelphia.

McGarry, J. (2015) 'Consociational Theory, Self Determination Disputes and Territorial Pluralism' in Basta, K., McGarry, J., & Simeon, R. (eds.), *Territorial Pluralism: Managing Differences in Multinational States*, UBC Press, Vancouver & Toronto.

McGarry, J. and Loizides, N. (2015) 'Power-Sharing in a Re-United Cyprus: Centripetal Coalitions vs. Proportional Sequential Coalitions.' *International Journal of Constitutional Law* 13 (4): 847–872.

McGarry, J., & O'Leary, B. (1993) *The Politics of Ethnic Conflict Regulation: Case Studies of Protracted Ethnic Conflicts*, Routledge, London.

McGarry, J., & O'Leary, B. (1995) *Explaining Northern Ireland: Broken Images*, Blackwell, Oxford.

McGarry, J., & O'Leary, B. (2004) *The Northern Ireland Conflict: Consociational Engagements*, Oxford University Press, Oxford.

McGarry, J., & O'Leary, B. (2006) 'Consociational Theory, Northern Ireland's Conflict, and its Agreement. Part 2: What Critics of Consociation Can Learn from Northern Ireland.' *Government and Opposition* 41 (2), 249–277.

McGarry, J., & O'Leary, B. (2009) 'Must Pluri-national Federations Fail?' *Ethnopolitics* 8 (1): 5–25.

Nordlinger, E. (1972) *Conflict Regulation in Divided Societies*, Center for International Affairs, Harvard, Cambridge, MA.

O'Leary, B. (1989) 'The Limits to Coercive Consociationalism in Northern Ireland.' *Political Studies* 37 (4): 562–588.

Reilly, B. (2002) 'Electoral Systems for Divided Societies.' *Journal of Democracy* 13 (2) April: 157–170.

Reilly, B. (2012) 'Institutional Designs for Diverse Democracies: Consociationalism, Centripetalism and Communalism Compared.' *European Political Science* 11 (2): 259–270.

Steiner, J. (1971) 'The Principles of Majority and Proportionality' *British Journal of Political Science* 1 (1): 63–70.

Taylor, R. (2009) 'The Injustice of a Consociational Solution to the Northern Ireland Problem' in Taylor, R. (ed.), *Consociational Theory: McGarry & O'Leary and the Northern Ireland Conflict*. Routledge, Abingdon.

Tonge, J. (2014) *Comparative Peace Processes*, Polity Press, Cambridge

1 Devolution and power-sharing in Northern Ireland

Northern Ireland has been at the centre of debates on political institution building in divided societies for many years, especially with regard to the benefits or drawbacks of power-sharing based on consociational political institutions. This was marked by two general phases. During the 1970s and into the 1980s, there was significant opposition from within the unionist community to the very concept of power-sharing. Democracy was conceived in majoritarian terms as it operated in the Westminster model and prior to devolution being granted to Scotland, Wales or Northern Ireland in the 1990s. Under this model of representative government, the party with the largest number of seats generally formed a single-party government or voluntary coalition administration. The concept of power-sharing was publicly repudiated by mainstream unionist politicians during this period as being anti-democratic or evidence of sympathy to Irish nationalism. Former Ulster Unionist Party MP Enoch Powell referred to 'that abominable absurdity of power-sharing, intolerable to any good democrat', during a debate in the House of Commons in 1978 on the renewal of emergency legislation to continue direct rule from Westminster.[1] Speaking in the same parliamentary debate, Bill Craig, MP for East Belfast and leader of the Vanguard Unionist Party, commented, 'There can be no parliamentary government in Northern Ireland that is not based on majority rule. The sooner that lesson is taken on board by all concerned, the better it will be for those who genuinely seek peace and stability.'[2] During this period in the Northern Ireland conflict, phrases such as 'power-sharing' and 'devolution' were loaded with political tension as they acted as coded signals for wider unionist and nationalist opposition over constitutional reform and control. The exception to this came during the 1973–1974 period with the emergence of the Sunningdale Agreement in 1973 and subsequent Power-Sharing Executive in 1974, when moderate unionists led by the former Northern Ireland prime minister Brian Faulkner went into devolved government with moderate nationalist parties and the non-aligned Alliance Party on a power-sharing basis. This initiative disintegrated shortly afterwards due to unionist opposition, and set the tone for future political attitudes towards devolved government for the rest of that decade.

Times change, of course, and this eventually moved into a second phase, where unionists came to accept power-sharing in the context of a broader peace process during the 1990s. This moved in parallel with the progress of the multi-party negotiations during the 1990s that culminated in the Belfast/Good Friday Agreement[3] (GFA) in 1998. At this point, the principle of devolved government based on power-sharing was overtaken by arguments over how this should be done, which parties should be involved in the sharing of power and the particular modalities linked to the operation of the new institutions. Unionists moved forwards on the basis of sharing power with the moderate Social Democratic and Labour Party (SDLP), rather than with the more radical Sinn Fein. Eventually, in 2007, following further periods of negotiation, unionists finally agreed to share power with Sinn Fein under the rules agreed in the Good Friday Agreement reached in 1998 and as amended in the St Andrews Agreement of 2006.

Since this point, there has been an energetic debate, both at party political and scholarly levels, as to whether the power-sharing structures are working effectively, or whether alternative approaches to the devolution of power would be preferable. The tensions between advocates/critical admirers and scholarly opponents of the GFA have circulated for a number of years and remain unresolved. The former claim the system provides minority safeguards against domination by the majority, while offering incentives for cross-community co-operation. The latter argue that this form of accommodationist power-sharing enshrines sectarian divisions in government and ultimately precludes cross-community co-operation or effective reconciliation (Horowitz, 2002; Taylor, 2009).

On the one hand (and notwithstanding their collapse following the 2 March 2017 Assembly Election), the region's power-sharing institutions have been relatively successful in securing political stability since 1998, despite the intermittent setbacks. Northern Ireland's d'Hondt system, which entitles the main parties to automatic representation in government on the basis of their electoral strength, is also critically important for consociational theory and is considered an attractive option in ongoing negotiations in Nepal, Cyprus and Colombia, among other countries. Yet in the eyes of its critics, Northern Ireland's 'government without opposition' form of power-sharing has been unable to build sufficient political legitimacy or transcend its deep inter-communal divisions.

Looking at the history of power-sharing in Northern Ireland for the past two decades as well as drawing on the private members' Opposition Reform Bill, which passed into legislation in March 2016, we focus on the empirical and normative challenges associated with re-negotiating the practice of consociational government in deeply divided societies. The desire for such re-negotiation emerges both from disagreement and conflict over the workings of such structures as well as the inevitable political evolution of these regions over time. Recent evidence from Northern Ireland demonstrates the limits of formal approaches to institutional change and highlights the need for informal practices to move in tandem with statutory reform in a contested political space. Northern Ireland demonstrates that power-sharing can evolve and mutate beyond its original design in response to the changing political context, and via a combination of formal and informal processes.

This chapter (along with the others in this volume) suggests that there is viable political space to be occupied, that bridges between the binary points of advocacy of power-sharing on the one hand and rejection of it on the other, as the basis for political settlements within divided societies. We offer the idea that there is a fluid boundary between the accommodationist approach of consociationalism and the integrationist model that denies the utility of power-sharing as a route to the peaceful transformation of violent conflict in deeply divided societies. The Northern Ireland case demonstrates that the ambitions of consociational power-sharing went far beyond an accommodationist vision in theory, but have been pulled towards this in practice.

The chapter connects to the others in this volume across three key areas: firstly, it provides an analysis of the formal and informal evolution of power-sharing and the combination of these patterns on the operation of the political institutions in the region. Secondly, the chapter provides empirical detail on the nature and functionality of a proportional political system in contrast to disproportional systems considered in other chapters. Thirdly, the chapter assesses the ways in which power-sharing in Northern Ireland has been affected by both endogenous and exogenous dynamics. The endogenous aspect relates to the internal political relationships between the main political parties and their wider electoral support. The exogenous dynamics are provided by the role of the UK and Irish governments on the operation of the political institutions and especially, by the UK referendum on membership of the European Union on 23 June 2016 and the aftermath of that vote. As with the other nations discussed in this volume, this changing external environment has had significant impacts on how power-sharing is understood in Northern Ireland and this will continue to affect how the institutions evolve over time.

Before looking at these themes, however, it is first important to assess the nature of power-sharing in Northern Ireland and the utility of the political institutions that emerged from the Good Friday Agreement after 1998.

Good Friday reconsidered

In institutional terms, the Good Friday Agreement combined elements of both classic and liberal consociationalism. Associated with Arend Lijphart (1977, 2004), consociationalism in its classic form emphasises community rights and minority vetoes; in Northern Ireland, this takes the form of community designation and cross-community voting. Following elections, Members of the Legislative Assembly (MLAs) have to designate themselves as unionists or nationalists in order to operate the cross-community power-sharing principles within the political system. A default classification of 'Others' is available for those unwilling to designate themselves as part of one or the other of the ethnonational groups. Approved bills require the concurrent majority consent of both community blocks represented in the Legislative Assembly. At the same time, through the d'Hondt mechanism, membership in the Executive is automatically determined by electoral strength. Until the last mandate that began after the assembly elections of 6 May 2016, this included all political groups reaching the minimum threshold of representation in the assembly (McGarry & O'Leary, 2004; McEvoy, 2014). While the last mandate ended prematurely, due to the resignation of the deputy First Minister Martin McGuinness (now deceased) causing an Assembly Election on 2 March 2017, the May 2016 mandate is, at the time of writing, the last fully operational period of the political system in NI.

With its use of the d'Hondt system to allocate seats in the Executive, power-sharing in Northern Ireland has been described as a novel and liberal form of consociationalism (McCulloch, 2013; McGarry, et al., 2001). For one thing, there are no fixed posts assigned to specific ethnic or religious groups, as in the Lebanese form of consociationalism, nor are there provisions for equal numbers of ministers from each main community, as in Belgium, nor are there separate electoral rolls, as in South Tyrol or the 1960 Cypriot constitution (McGarry & Loizides, 2015). For another, by including all major parties in the allocation of cabinet seats (up to May 2016), Northern Ireland's d'Hondt system eliminated a problematic and time-consuming aspect of consociationalism, that of forming inter-ethnic majority coalitions. This straightforward and inclusive mechanism led Northern Ireland to an unprecedented level of political stability from 2007 to 2017, though this remains brittle and subject to intermittent crises, as outlined below.

In general, the critical challenge for divided societies is to institutionalise a broadly inclusive, functional and legitimate coalition representing all groups that is not significantly different from the composition of their respective populations. Although there are several examples – from Belgium, Switzerland and, of course, Northern Ireland – the latter model is the most formalised, quicker to form and suitable for low-trust environments.

More specifically, Northern Ireland stands out across alternative power-sharing models in combining inclusivity and proportionality, with automaticity in the formation of its executive (McEvoy 2015). This unique feature links government formation to an arithmetic algorithm, but at the same time, it disincentivises long-term coalition strategy-building over policy issues or even an outline consensus over a programme for government. In other words, parties can remain in a competitive oppositional mode rather than moving towards a co-operative or partnership relationship, because they have little need to reach policy agreements before taking office. Rather, they may have a greater need to emphasise what divides them than what unites them, continuing on from recent election campaigns, as access to governmental office is not contingent on reaching policy agreements with other political parties. This system therefore provides few incentives for parties to build coalitions with prospective partners in government over policy agendas. In practice, this has led to an efficient technical mechanism for appointing the Executive from the elected Legislative Assembly, but not always with great clarity over policy priorities or political direction once formed.

Framing the Northern Ireland context

Northern Ireland's 'peace process' has lasted for a generation; 2017 marked the 24th anniversary of the Downing Street Declaration, which cemented the foundation for the joint approach to the conflict by successive British and Irish governments, and the 23rd anniversary of the main paramilitary ceasefires. The 20th anniversary of the Good Friday Agreement, which framed the broad political and constitutional geometry for today's system of devolved government, will occur in April 2018. We have had a system of devolved power-sharing in Northern Ireland for a generation (albeit with several periods of hiatus and inertia, including the present one, in the wake of the 2 March 2017 Assembly Election). Given this generational time frame, and on the cusp of the 20th anniversary of the GFA, it seems an appropriate time to reflect on the experience of power-sharing in Northern Ireland.

The key questions to ask are: firstly, to what extent has the consociational architecture successfully managed the conflict in Northern Ireland? Secondly, what more might be done to consolidate its strengths and remedy its weaknesses? Such determinations depend, of course, on what benchmarks we use to evaluate success and failure, including institutional robustness, the curbing of violence and reasonable levels of functionality in the political system and its associated institutions, as well as broader issues of public support.

Simply stated, the GFA recognised the political realities of enduring ethno-nationalist political divisions and broader politico-cultural sectarianism, and built a range of political institutions based on consociational democracy to manage these tensions and disagreements – leaving intractable ones out. It was an institutional bargain between the main representatives of the unionist and nationalist communities. And it was an effective one – recognised as such by 71% of the electorate in the May 1998 referendum (Mitchell, 2001: 30). This electoral result legitimised the implementation of the GFA, but the devolved structure was not so successful – suspended four times between 1999 and 2002, with a hiatus from 2002 to 2007. At the time of writing (September 2017), another period of political instability has been generated as a result of disagreements between Sinn Fein and the DUP before and after the Assembly Election of 2 March 2017. It is currently unclear if the parties will return to devolved government, or whether direct rule will be restored in the absence of power-sharing structures operating at Stormont. The outcome of the Westminster General Election on 8 June 2017 may act as a further barrier to the restoration of power-sharing in NI as the DUP agreed to a command and supply arrangement with the Conservative Party government in London. The 'deal' between the DUP and the current government is unlikely to augment the confidence of the political actors in NI, or the already strained relations between the DUP and Sinn Fein.

As the bumpy road suggests, despite achieving the support of both unionists and nationalists in 1998, the peace process has faced repeated challenges, including the ambivalent commitment of unionist parties and their broader electorates, the slow pace of change evidenced through the decommissioning of paramilitary weapons and the inability to deal effectively with the past. In the final analysis, the record is mixed – as we might expect of a society coming out of political violence.

Despite the setbacks highlighted above, the majority of political parties in Northern Ireland have come to agree on a political geometry based on power-sharing and an Irish dimension. Today, the comparison of unionist political voices with their predecessors from the 1970s and 1980s, provided at the beginning of this chapter, is stark. All of the main unionist political parties accept (and even embrace) the concept of power-sharing and devolution, and they mostly find the Irish dimension as set out in the GFA unproblematic as well.

The problems that divide the unionist and nationalist political parties and their respective electorates are defined more in terms of identity politics and the difficulty of coming to terms with legacy issues from the conflict than with top-line constitutional issues such as power-sharing or institutions that connect Northern Ireland and the Irish Republic.

A caveat to add here is that the UK referendum on EU membership held on 23 June 2016 holds the potential for the constitutional issue to re-emerge as a barrier to power-sharing being re-established or functioning smoothly in Northern Ireland. Despite the Brexit issue and the current hiatus in the operation of the devolved institutions, power-sharing in Northern Ireland has played a large role in reducing political violence, (especially fatalities), maintaining political stability and promoting the region's economic viability. Overall, the political institutions in Northern Ireland have done well in their short-term conflict management goals, despite being less impressive in transforming the wider conflict. The institutions clearly need to do more to convert short-term gains into longer-term sustainable relationships. If this is not addressed, advances risk being lost.[4] At the same time, many feel that more ambitious institutional proposals for change, such as John McCallister's Assembly Reform Act of March 2016, risks jeopardising the progress already made. This is a critical dilemma facing Northern Ireland and other post-conflict societies, including post-Dayton Bosnia or post-apartheid South Africa, where conflict-mitigating institutions have performed well in some areas but not in others. In all cases, major constitutional revisions seem necessary, but are dangerous and difficult to achieve without risking instability and mistrust, with people on both sides of a conflict fearing the peace process is being manipulated by one ethnonational group to the disadvantage of the other.

Simply stated, the GFA recognised the political realities of enduring ethnonational political divisions and broader politico-cultural sectarianism and built a range of political institutions based on consociational democracy that could manage these tensions and disagreements – leaving intractable ones out. It was an institutional bargain between the main representatives of the unionist and nationalist communities; and it was an effective one – recognised as such by 71% of the electorate in the May 1998 referendum (Mitchell, 2001, 30). This significant level of public endorsement disguised the fact that the unionist community was very divided over the terms of the GFA, which led to acrimony over its implementation and mistrust over longer-term motives on both sides. In truth, the GFA was always different things to different constituencies, with unionist and nationalist political parties emphasising different aspects rather than regarding it a joint enterprise. These alternative readings of power-sharing and ongoing mistrust between the main unionist and nationalist communities and their political representatives led to endemic instability and the periodic breakdown of devolution four times between 1999 and 2002 – with a long interregnum between 2002 and 2007 when direct rule from London returned, while the parties attempted to negotiate their way out of an impasse over sharing power.

The political system looked to have overcome its endemic instability with ten years of unbroken devolved government from 2007 to 2017, though following the 2 March 2017 Assembly Election we have entered another phase of uncertainty, with no power-sharing in operation, inter-party talks ongoing and the main financial and political decisions being taken by the Secretary of State and by civil servants, rather than by locally elected politicians. For most of this period, there has been a general inability within the main unionist and nationalist communities to view power-sharing or political interests as being inter-dependent. Instead, the main political parties have co-operated in government (when they managed to form one) but did so in an adversarial relationship which constantly pulled them back from areas of co-operation, especially those that intersected with the ethnonational dynamics of the conflict. The impression given, therefore, is that they share power because they are *forced to do so* – rather than because they *want to do so*. This would be relatively unproblematic if they could do this effectively – but that has not been the experience since the devolved structures were first established in 1999.

The difficult behavioural relations between the DUP and SF declined steadily during Peter Robinson's period as DUP leader and first minister from 2008 to 2014, and worsened under Arlene Foster, his successor as first minister, to the point that former Deputy First Minister Martin McGuinness resigned from his position, precipitating the March 2017 Assembly Election. Into all of this, the Brexit process has brought a structural barrier, as the DUP and SF (and their supporters) are on opposite sides of the argument over whether and how the UK should leave the European Union. Northern Ireland, as a region, chose to remain in the EU (by a vote of 56% to 44%) but is being treated as an integral part of the UK in the Brexit negotiations by the government in London. This has started to become fused with the old constitutional question over whether NI is an integral part of the UK or deserves to have a right to self-determination. This is not without some irony, as Sinn Fein, which oppose partition and argue for Irish reunification, have insisted on the right of the electorate in Northern Ireland to exercise self-determination over the Brexit issue. The DUP, meanwhile, traditionally a supporter of political devolution and majoritarian democracy in Northern Ireland, sublimated the majority view of the NI electorate in the Brexit referendum under a desire for an integrated process within the UK as a whole.

However, despite the current problems caused by the Brexit process, poor relations between the DUP and Sinn Fein and the absence of a functioning devolved executive, the benefits that consociational power-sharing has delivered to NI should not be undervalued. The majority of political parties and those voting for them across the unionist and nationalist spectrum now broadly agree on power-sharing with an Irish dimension. Today there is no apparent desire to argue for an *alternative to power-sharing* and all parties seem committed in principle to the restoration of devolved government, though differences remain in practice over the terms under which that should happen. All of these issues and achievements are linked to the power-sharing structures established in the wake of the GFA in 1998 and to subsequent negotiations which refined the original agreement.

While the concept of consociational power-sharing is now broadly accepted in NI, it remains chronically dysfunctional and there is an urgent need to improve its institutional resilience and its capacity to generate incentives for co-operation across the ethnonational divide. Some observers have argued that the current phase of political devolution in Northern Ireland established in the wake of the GFA in 1998 is actually coming to an end. This view is particularly prevalent in some journalistic circles, where scepticism has been the dominant attitude for some time – arguably for all of the time. Belfast-based journalist Alex Kane referred to the nascent devolved government as being 'a well funded stalemate' in August 2017.[5]

Even if such voices are cast as being cynical doom-merchants, the institutions of devolved government in Northern Ireland should clearly be working more effectively than they are. To say that power-sharing has delivered stability since 1998, that the institutions have survived for almost two decades and the number of conflict-related fatalities has decreased dramatically over the period is not sufficient. The success of devolved government in Northern Ireland needs to be benchmarked by something more than a basic functionality of the institutions and lack of killing outside them. The power-sharing institutions need to promote 'bridging' social capital between unionist and nationalist communities and positive incentives for ethnonational co-operation. The obvious absence of this has resulted in a lack of common purpose at the top of government over recent years, leading to the implosion of the devolved structures, the Assembly Election of 2 March 2017 and the inability of the main two parties to go back into government together. The current standoff between Sinn Fein and the DUP is resulting in political and economic disadvantage, both with regard to protecting Northern Ireland's interests in the Brexit negotiations as well as decisions over the spending of public money in areas such as health and education. However, there are few signs that either party is suffering electorally for their inability to restore the devolved institutions, and arguably they have both strengthened their positions rather than weakened them.

It is easy to say that change is needed but more difficult to design and even harder to negotiate. Exactly how can the devolved political structures deliver more effective governance, within a broader conflict transformation framework, that combines effectiveness with the sort of cross-community guarantees that must be maintained in the system? It is clear from events leading up to and following the 2 March 2017 Assembly Election that the main parties currently do not trust each other nor share much sense of joint enterprise in terms of the ethnonational divide, and that these positions are also largely shared – and underwritten – by the electorate in Northern Ireland. Yet at the same time, power-sharing provides the most obvious and also the most accepted framework for mediating these differences and, in time, overcoming them.

In 2013, the Northern Ireland Executive and Assembly Review Committee reported on the operation of d'Hondt, Community Designation and Provisions for Opposition. The committee asked what could both improve the functionality and quality of the political system and also secure broad support for it (Northern Ireland Assembly, 2013). In the remaining sections of this chapter, we examine the transformative potential of the consociational model in Northern Ireland and across divided societies more generally. The argument presented is that while the current arrangements in Northern Ireland have provided an effective conflict management approach for the province's devolved institutions, the provision for a formal opposition, and other symbolic alterations linked to the establishment of co–first minister positions and community designation labelling, can further assist the process of transformative change.

Governing without opposition in Northern Ireland

The operation of the devolved institutions proposed by the Good Friday Agreement has enhanced political stability since 1998 (especially from 2007 to 2017) but so far it has been unable to transform wider conflict relationships, risking the long-term sustainability of the institutions. There are only so many periods of suspension, temporary direct rule and negotiation about reconstituting power-sharing that can be sustained before such a process loses credibility and viability. Northern Ireland would appear to be at such a tipping point at the time of writing (November 2017) which is why urgent attention to address the weaknesses of the system is needed. Several phases of talks between the DUP and Sinn Fein have ended in failure and led to a slide towards direct rule from Westminster.

The region has embraced power-sharing as a core principle of government, yet has evidently experienced a crisis-ridden political system. On the one hand, this could be attributed to the coercive origins of power-sharing in Northern Ireland and the role of external actors in providing not only incentives but also 'threats, particularly that if unionists did not cooperate with nationalists they could lose even more policy-making influence in the future' (Tannam, 2012: 51. See also O'Leary, 1989). On the other, the automaticity of the d'Hondt Executive has enabled broad participation (including SF) that creates an incentive for an end to violence through political inclusivity (Whiting, 2016). In broader terms, Northern Ireland has developed a novel and attractive model for local democracy in divided societies, aiming at guarantees of cross-community inclusion and proportionality. On the other hand, because they are automatically included in decision-making, Northern Ireland's main parties have failed to develop a consensual political culture, prioritizing zero-sum, intra-ethnic populism over winning long-term coalition partners. The examples below suggest that the province still lacks adequate levels of collective endeavour to prevent short-term difficulties becoming a longer-term crisis of political viability for the power-sharing system. By 2017 the mistrust and enmity between the main political parties had become too strong, and the wider context was one where the Deputy First Minister, Martin McGuinness, was in the grip of a terminal illness, and the Brexit issue had spliced a major structural division into the already dysfunctional relationship between the DUP (which supported Brexit) and SF (which opposed it).

After a generation, the devolved institutions in Northern Ireland remain inherently unstable and fragile. They have survived, though not in a manner that has made them more robust or effective in managing or mediating community sectarianism and issues relating to contested ethnonational identities in Northern Ireland. This fragility was underlined after the 6 May 2016 Assembly Election, when it became clear that appointing a minister to the justice portfolio would not be straightforward. A number of possible candidates were interviewed by the first and deputy first ministers, including Steven Agnew of the Green Party, before Independent unionist MLA Claire Sugden was appointed to the role. Neither the DUP nor SF (or their respective electorates) had sufficient confidence in the other party to accept this sensitive portfolio going to either a unionist or nationalist (eliminating four of the five main political parties). Sugden was an inexperienced appointment but a pragmatic one, and although her being chosen solved the immediate problem, it highlighted a deeper malaise in the political system in Northern Ireland. If there was such mistrust over the appointment of the justice minister between the main *partners* in government, then the chances of the Executive effectively tackling the outstanding problems linked to ongoing sectarianism and community division were arguably dim from the outset.

The delay and eventual appointment of Sugden as justice minister in 2016 highlighted the fact that fragility and instability have been endemic features of devolution in Northern Ireland since 1998. The power-sharing structures that were eventually established in 1999 provided no incentives to remain outside the governing multi-party coalition, if a party qualified for a ministerial position in the Executive through the d'Hondt mechanism. The result was that over time, parties found themselves in government with little common agenda, with the smaller parties feeling marginalised and the larger parties frustrated by the ambivalent attitudes of their 'partners' in government. In blunt terms, the power-sharing system allowed everyone to be in government, but provided little visible opposition or alternatives to the governing status quo.

Opposition to power-sharing has been supplied by an array of uncoordinated sources, but these have had little ideological or organisational coherence and have evolved in response to the absence of a formal system and any dedicated resources. The Democratic Unionist Party (DUP) initially played an oppositional role by rejecting the GFA and campaigning against it in the May 1998 referendum. Members took their seats in the Executive when the devolved structures were established in 1999, but they did not attend its meetings, rotated their two ministerial positions and generally attempted to disrupt the new system. The DUP claimed this was a responsible form of opposition that would hold the Ulster Unionist Party (UUP) to account in its dealings with Sinn Fein, but it represented opposition to the *existence* of the system, not a desire to improve its functionality. As First Minister Peter Robinson recollects: 'In the end we opted to rewrite the rules of government and create a new category of Minister. We became Ministers in Opposition' (Cochrane, 2013, 211).

When devolution was restored in 2007, with the DUP and SF replacing the UUP and SDLP, a new form of *ad hoc* opposition crept into the political system. Although the UUP and SDLP were part of the Executive, they frequently adopted an oppositional attitude within it, alleging the two largest parties (DUP and SF) were subverting the spirit of the GFA as a grand coalition by presiding over a sectarian division of power and resources. Both the SDLP and UUP frequently opposed and undermined decisions made by the Executive while they were members of it, including refusing to support the Programme for Government (PfG). Ultimately, both of these parties opted to leave the government and go into formal opposition – though at different times, for different reasons and without much sense of co-operation or joint purpose.

Overall, neither government nor opposition have been able to develop a common set of objectives. The post-GFA political structures have brought stability and a relative absence of violence, but dealing with the past, addressing identity issues, tackling social exclusion and growing Protestant working-class alienation, remain elusive goals (Cochrane, 2012; Gilligan, 2008; Todd & Ruane, 2010; Nolan 2014). The wider argument here is that the institutions need to do more than simply survive in order to evolve in a way that connects elite accommodation to broader community-based acceptance. McCrudden et al. (2016) are correct to point out that Northern Ireland's institutions need stability, but they also need credibility to ensure their long term survival and relevance.

While much of the literature focuses on political institution-building as a key element of a broader movement to achieve stable government and sustainable non-violence, this political engineering has to be supplemented with wider attitudinal change in society. The GFA went beyond the narrow containment agenda of conservative conflict management approaches that focus primarily on stability. Its ambitions far surpassed the containment of violence or the management of conflict to simply minimise casualties – what used to be euphemistically referred to as 'an acceptable level of violence'. It provided instead the foundations for an ethnonational accommodation between Ulster unionism and Irish nationalism that went to the root causes of the political conflict. The aspirations of the GFA and subsequent iterations, such as the St Andrews Agreement in 2006, the Stormont House Agreement in 2014 and the Fresh Start deal in 2015, were designed to provide a holistic framework for underlying conflict relationships. The 'triple-lock' mechanism of the GFA also situated it beyond a traditional top-down conflict management approach, as the agreement was put to dual referenda in Northern Ireland and the Irish Republic, won the majority support of local political elites and gained assent in the respective parliaments in London and Dublin. Thus, in addition to the more traditional top-down formal political process, the GFA had a bottom-up inclusive component in an effort to maximise community buy-in and minimise 'spoiler' destabilisation.

However, while its initial aspirations included a comprehensive settlement of the conflict, its actual operation has worked more towards containment. The chronic instability of the political process between 1999 and 2007 (and as experienced after the 2 March 2017 Assembly Election and the 8 June Westminster General Election) has fuelled criticism of the capacity and viability of the power-sharing system itself. The stability achieved after the 2007 phase of devolved government has not been supplemented by the increased credibility of the political institutions or those involved in them.

The rest of this chapter considers some informal refinements to the institutions that may have the capacity to improve urgently needed political stability and build long-term transformative capacity in Northern Ireland's power-sharing system.

The case for and against reform of power-sharing principles

Not everyone supports the need for reform of the political institutions in Northern Ireland, or believes that formal or informal changes (such as the provision of a recognised opposition to the Executive), will make it more robust. The devolved government in Northern Ireland, it was argued (at least up until the institutions collapsed in 2017), successfully managed the previously unbridgeable ethnonational cleavage, providing much-needed stability. There were, of course, tensions, incompatibilities and crises, but these were no greater than in other polities, and the devolved system should not be held to utopian benchmarks of governance not observable elsewhere. According to critical admirers of consociationalism, modelling showed that the system was stable, or at least no worse than in comparable regions (McCrudden et al.: 2016). This perspective appears a little strained currently (November 2017) as the devolved institutions have been in abeyance since the former Deputy First Minister Martin McGuinness resigned in January 2017. The Assembly Election that this precipitated in March 2017 failed to resolve the outstanding problems, and interparty talks to reconstitute the Executive fell apart without agreement being reached in the summer of 2017. By November, the British government had begun taking back political control and moving incrementally towards the introduction of direct rule from Westminster. In light of these developments, the argument that the institutions are working effectively (or as effectively as should be expected) is difficult to justify.

The second argument against making changes to devolved government in NI (such as provision for a formal opposition to the Executive) is technical, but important in the re-conceptualization of the micro-institutional aspects of power-sharing in deeply divided societies. Those opposed to the introduction of a formal opposition to devolved government in Northern Ireland claim that it is a closed system whose constituent parts are inter-connected and thus co-dependent. Thus, while one element, such as the capacity for opposition, may not have an optimal design, it is the price that has to be paid for significant gains elsewhere. Moreover, performing surgery in one area could potentially damage the integrity and functionality of the overall system of government. The argument here is that opposition was built into the fabric of devolution and expressed through the statutory committee structure, even if it did not play a more direct role, as in adversarial systems such as Westminster. The statutory committee structure of the assembly has accounted for an oppositional function in its requirement that committee chairs and deputy chairs be drawn from parties other than that of the minister concerned, thus encouraging broader institutional scrutiny and offsetting the absence of dedicated opposition within the system. A related argument was that nothing compelled political parties to participate in the Executive if they did not wish to, and all parties were at liberty to leave and become an opposition if they wanted to do so – as the UUP, the SDLP and the Alliance Party eventually did in 2016. Thus, the multi-party coalition characterising the previous mandates prior to 2016 was a consequence of political choice and party behaviour, not a requirement of the system *per se* (McCrudden, McGarry, O'Leary, and Schwartz, 2013: 231).

However, structures also shape and frame political choices, and it could be argued that until recently, the lack of obvious incentives for parties to do anything but take up their seats in the Power-Sharing Executive gave them Hobson's choice, not a meaningful one. It is not ideal to use the committee system as a surrogate for a co-ordinated system of opposition, and the suggestion that

Northern Ireland does not need one or cannot have one because of its ethnonational cleavage needs greater substantiation. While the committees have provided useful scrutiny in the NI Assembly, this is more of an oversight function and, crucially, is not capable of providing alternative policy platforms that parties can develop and voters can choose between at election time.

Introducing the 'conventional dichotomy' – as in most contemporary democracies – between a government and a formal opposition offers several potential benefits to political institutions. This was created in embryonic form after the 2016 Assembly Election, but failed to gain traction or coherence before the institutions collapsed in 2017. The main reasons for this were twofold. Firstly, the parties that went into opposition did not adequately define a strategic direction that would establish areas of co-operation between them to the governing Executive. There was at best an uneasy co-operation between the SDLP, the UUP and the Alliance Party and more often a lack of coherence in responses to key policy issues. There was thus little unity of purpose or added value – which, given the fact that the UUP was fundamentally a unionist party and the SDLP a nationalist one, is not surprising. Secondly, the mandate following the 2016 Assembly Election was too short for these opposition parties to really make a significant mark on the working of the institutions or on public consciousness. The eight-month period from the Assembly Election in May 2016 till the resignation of Martin McGuiness in January 2017 was too brief for the opposition voices to develop a coherent strategic direction or a significant record of achievement.

Should devolution be revived in Northern Ireland, we are unlikely to see formal UUP-SDLP coalitions in the short term, but if the UUP and SDLP opt to go into opposition in the future, the parties may build a portfolio of cross-ethnic co-operation on an issue-by-issue basis over time. This was not done adequately when both parties went into opposition following the May 2016 Assembly Election – resulting in a fractured, incoherent and ineffective opposition voice that was unable to establish itself as an alternative to the SF-DUP government in the short period that the assembly mandate lasted. But this failure may serve as a valuable lesson to smaller parties looking for a relevant political role in the future. Despite its limitations, this move to opposition did demonstrate the capacity of the consociational political system in NI to incorporate more centripetalist features, as the parties in opposition were not bound by parallel consent or community designation.

Formal and informal approaches to political reform: Advancing consociationalism?

The political institutions in Northern Ireland are evolving through a combination of formal and informal processes, converting the consociational model from one of government without formal opposition, in the 2011–2016 mandate, to one of government with formal opposition(s), in the 2016–2017 mandate. We will have to wait to see whether there is a further mandate following the March 2017 Assembly Election, and how opposition features in any subsequent power-sharing systems.

The 2016–2017 experience of opposition could be considered as a pilot exercise that highlighted some areas where more attention is required. In reality the 2016–2017 mandate resulted in multiple oppositions to the power-sharing government. There were two formal oppositions (UUP and SDLP), as well as the Alliance Party and a range of minor parties, all in opposition. This alone demonstrates the capacity for political evolution in Northern Ireland and sends a message about the adaptability of the consociational model for deeply divided societies. It certainly was not a perfect arrangement and arguably was not an especially effective one – but it did demonstrate how political structures can adapt and evolve organically over time, in line with inter-party consensus, in ways not envisaged in 1998.

This particular evolution can be traced to a mix of formal and informal efforts to reform the political institutions, in response to the recognition that while stability had been achieved, the devolved structures were struggling to work smoothly. The inter-party disagreements over the Programme for Government, welfare reforms (which the DUP supported and Sinn Fein opposed) and legacy issues relating to the conflict precipitated numerous crisis talks between the main parties (Stormont House Agreement [SHA] in 2014 and Fresh Start in 2015). These talks produced informal agreements between the DUP and Sinn Fein that affected the nature of the political institutions and the rules under which power-sharing operated. The SHA of December 2014 was a direct consequence of the inability of the main parties, in particular SF and the DUP, to reach agreement over welfare reform and a range of other devolved policy matters. It stipulated the circumstances for the establishment of a formal opposition and incentives to enable this:

> Arrangements will be put in place by the Assembly by March 2015 to enable those parties which would be entitled to ministerial positions in the Executive, but choose not to take them up, to be recognised as an official opposition and to facilitate their work. These measures will include: a) Provision for financial and research assistance . . . and b) Designated speaking rights including the opportunity to ask questions and table business sufficient to permit the parties to discharge their opposition duties.
>
> (Stormont House Agreement, 23 December 2014: 13)

This agreement exemplified the capacity for informal reform of the political institutions through inter-party dialogue and consensus building, the basis on which the GFA was founded, rather than through formal statutory legislation.

In a parallel development, the former UUP MLA John McCallister[6] introduced an Opposition Reform Private Members Bill in September 2015 to pursue a formal statutory route to institutional reform.[7] The intention was to provide statutory provision for a recognised opposition in the assembly and to confer formal rights on that opposition, mainly with respect to parliamentary time and financial resources. The bill sought to enhance collective decision-making within the assembly and the Executive by ending the formal cross-community requirement facilitated through 'community designation'[8] of MLAs. It also proposed a reform of the Petitions of Concern mechanism for blocking legislation and converting the Office of First Minister and Deputy First Minister into a collective Joint First Minister title. The bill was brought forward by McCallister because of the endemic instability of the political institutions and the inability of the main parties to deliver policy objectives addressing the key economic and social problems facing Northern Ireland:

> We have come to the point at which, in effect, we either reform the Assembly or it will fail. . . . We all know the reason why the Assembly and these institutions are here: they were born out of the Belfast/Good Friday Agreement. . . . Does that mean that we want these institutions to be somehow frozen in time? Absolutely not. It was always envisaged that they would evolve. However, the broad principles of that agreement, about genuine power-sharing and inclusivity, are those that I voted for and still agree with and adhere to. It is about how we deliver that normalisation of our politics, where parties present costed, realistic manifestos before an election.
>
> (McCallister, 2015, Assembly Official Report)

This was a serious undertaking, not least because McCallister was an independent MLA attempting to navigate reactions to its contents that ranged from political ambivalence to outright hostility across both the DUP and SF. Accordingly, it was subject to a considerable degree of attentive scrutiny and debate, including an extension of the Committee Stage in October 2015 to facilitate a call for written stakeholder evidence, oral hearings and subsequent deliberation and amendment to the proposed legislation. The tone of the debate over the Bill was extremely obstructive. SF was implacably opposed to formal statutory reform and maintained consistent opposition to it throughout. Both SF and the SDLP were especially opposed to the bill's proposals for ending community designation, as they feared this contravened the cross-community power-sharing and proportionality principles of the Good Friday Agreement. Despite these and the numerous other objections to the bill, both in terms of its substantive content and the more technical mechanics of how it could work, it kept the issue of opposition and broader thinking about the evolution of the political system on the political agenda for the main parties. The move towards developing a recognised formal opposition to the power-sharing Executive was reinforced and reiterated following the Fresh Start Agreement of November 2015, which outlined the circumstances under which it could be introduced. The Fresh Start negotiations were themselves a result of the failure of the SHA to progress.

The agreement, reached essentially between SF and the DUP, restated the above section from the SHA on the establishment of an official opposition, but added more detail on the steps anticipated after the 2016 Assembly Election that would facilitate its introduction (*Fresh Start* Section F, 2015:55). The agreement also set out the envisaged ring-fenced speaking rights of an official opposition during plenary business, Executive Business debates and the prospect of 'opposition debates', subject to the agreement of the Speaker of the Assembly – in consultation with the Assembly Business Committee (ibid: 55–6).

SF was implacably opposed to statutory reform, opposing all 24 clauses of McCallister's bill during its committee stage – including one relating to reform of OFMDFM into an office of Joint First Ministers that SF had itself unilaterally and informally suggested to the DUP. However, Sinn Fein was more amenable to *informal change* via standing orders as mooted in the SHA and Fresh Start agreements.

When McCallister's bill was watered down and brought into line with Fresh Start, it passed into law, receiving Royal Assent on 23 March 2016, and setting up the possibility of *government with opposition* in future assembly mandates. The Assembly and Executive Reform (Assembly Opposition) Act 2016[9] differs substantially from McCallister's original bill, dropping key elements, such as the proposed changes to community designation, the reform of OFMDFM and the curbing of petitions of concern to block legislation. The act enshrined an 8% minimum threshold of seats in the assembly for parties to qualify for recognition as a formal opposition; in effect, such qualifying parties would have enhanced financial resources and more parliamentary time, so long as they did not take up ministerial office. The act stipulated that subsequent standing orders must make provision for an opposition member to be on the Business Committee. In addition, enhanced speaking rights for the opposition should be based on a minimum of 10 days per year being set aside for opposition business (Assembly and Executive Reform Act 2016: 2–3).

As McCallister's bill gained traction, several of the political parties began shifting their public positions on the issue of formal opposition. This was facilitated within the SDLP by the election of Colum Eastwood in 2015 to replace traditionalist Alisdair McDonnell. In his first address to the Annual Conference as new leader of the party, Eastwood significantly altered the party's policy: 'In the past this party has stayed within the Executive without signing up to a Programme for Government. That ends now. We will only enter the Executive if we can agree to a Programme for Government which actually meets the need of people in the North' (SDLP, 13 March 2016).[10] This commitment was underscored in the SDLP's manifesto for the 2016 Assembly Election, which hinted at the prospect of opposition in the next mandate:

> The SDLP are running for government. After the stagnation, government must now succeed. That is our ambition. We are also clear however that this will be the last Assembly mandate in which there will be no provision for an Opposition. That is why we have supported the efforts of others and proposed our own mechanisms to create a credible and robust role for an Opposition in the Assembly's structures.
>
> (SDLP Manifesto, *Build A Better Future*, 2016: 48)

For their part, the UUP withdrew from the Executive in 2014 before the incentives of formal opposition had been established, partly for reasons of perceived electoral advantage. This move, together with their manifesto and associated election campaign, made it clear that entering opposition was a realistic option if they could not agree with the PfG drawn up immediately after the election on 5 May:

> When the PfG is finalised, we will ask two key questions: Is it a progressive Programme for Government, of benefit to all the people; and have we sensed a collective political will around the table to deliver it? If the answer to either question is 'No', we will not re-join the Northern Ireland Executive, forming instead the first Official Opposition in the Northern Ireland Assembly.
>
> (UUP Manifesto, Make It Work, 2016: 5)

The 2016 NI Assembly Election and the debates preceding it on the desirability of formal and informal reform of the political institutions thus opened the door to a new phase, changing government without opposition into government with opposition – before the government itself disintegrated in January 2017 and into mutual recriminations after that.

It should be clear from all of this that consociationalism is not a closed loop, with conflict parties locked into static relationships of mutual inter-dependence and power-sharing. The political structures in Northern Ire-land have evolved over time through a combination of formal and informal reforms, with the move towards recognition of a formal opposition in the assembly indicative of the capacity of the political structures to adapt and change. The creation of a formalised opposition in 2016 provided a model (as yet improperly applied) for more structured and consistent scrutiny of the governing Executive. If power-sharing is restored to NI and parties opt to go back into opposition and do so with the intention of building a common agenda on key issues, this could, over time, help to distinguish between alternative political programmes and create more choice for the electorate within and across the existing ethnonational cleavage. Critics of the pre-2016 arrangements have argued in stakeholder evidence given to the Northern Ireland Assembly Review Committee that creating a formal opposition could build additional progressive dynamics into the political system, especially accountability and the capacity to develop alternative programmes for the government to offer greater electoral choice (Wilford, *Review of d'Hondt, Community Designation and Provisions for Opposi-tion*, 2013: 268). Others claimed that it was perverse to reward parties for opposing the political system rather than operating it. They suggested that this could create a status incommensurate with electoral support, something antithetical to the proportionality logic of the GFA's consociational arrange-ments (McCrudden et al., 2016). It certainly does demonstrate the capacity of consociationalism in NI to adapt over time and to blend informal and for-mal reforms that can incorporate centripetalist approaches to power-sharing.

Underlying some of the opposition to reform is a fear among many nation-alists that any tinkering with the political institutions to create more informal coalitions, particularly with respect to the cross-community power-sharing that enshrines mutual vetoes, would see unionist parties align with others to exclude Sinn Fein from government. John McCallister admitted this in the final stages before his Opposition Reform Bill was passed into legislation by the assembly in February 2016. He conceded that ending community designation did not inspire the confidence of the SDLP or SF: 'I would have liked to see changes on designation. We, as unionists, have to ask ourselves this: why is nationalism, as a collective, still so afraid of that change? As we want to develop, mature and see those changes over time, we have to look at how we progress that issue'.[11]

It is clear that unionists have so far been unable to allay nationalist fear that they will seek to impose their majority opinion if they get a chance to do so (as that was their experience from 1921 until this capacity was removed from unionists in 1972). Everything that has taken place over the last few years, including the current impasse between the DUP and Sinn Fein, is only likely to reinforce the nationalist view that unionists are emotionally challenged by the thought of sharing power with nationalists and need careful monitoring over the terms by which they do so. Evidence of this was provided at the end of August 2017 when former UUP Deputy Leader Lord Kilclooney (John Taylor) made a comment on social media that while nationalists deserved equal opportunities with unionists on an individual basis, they were not on an equal political footing as unionists were the majority community and nationalists the minority.[12] This provoked Sinn Fein's Mártín Ó Muilleoir to respond by saying: 'If I am not misinterpreting him really what he is saying is that we (nationalists) will have to stay at the back of the bus.'[13] Clearly nationalists continue to fear that unionists still have not reconciled themselves emotionally to sharing power and have to be held to the rules to avoid slipping back into their majoritarian tendencies, as experienced in the first phase of devolved government in NI from 1921 to 1972.

We recognise this nationalist concern about loosening the mutual vetoes in the power-sharing institutions and argue that the formal statutory approach, as represented in the McCallister bill, shaped the negative response of Sinn Fein. This approach linked the issue of formal opposition with a range of other proposed institutional changes, including ending community designation and Petitions of Concern within the assembly, and pursued them through formal legislative change. The fear of having unwieldy legislation foisted on it, being unable to frame and influence reform incrementally or to resist it if necessary, inspired Sinn Fein's implacable opposition to McCallister's bill and required its significant alteration as detailed below. Even the SDLP, which potentially stood to gain from the facilitation of a recognised opposition role, objected to key sections of the bill, *including amendments they themselves had introduced.* Ending community designation via formal statute was a step too far for the SDLP; they signed a Petition of Concern against this and other aspects of the bill in February 2016 (*Newsletter*, 2 February 2016).[14]

In contrast to the formal statutory approach, the pursuit of informal change in standing orders, developed by the political parties through consensus in inter-party negotiations such as SHA and Fresh Start, opened up a viable route for the development of opposition and smaller governing coalitions, while retaining proportionality and cross-community power-sharing in the political structures. This nuanced political system, driven by an organic connection between formal statutory change and informal convention derived through political negotiation, may eventually lead to the end of community designation in the Northern Ireland Assembly, but it need not necessarily do so, and this will emerge only if the main parties come to see such arrangements as attractive. In some ways this can be seen in parallel to the issue of eventual Irish reunification – it may happen but will only do so as a result of a collective buy-in by both unionist and nationalist communities and their political representatives.

For now, Northern Ireland's power-sharing model retains the political geometry established by the GFA of cross-community power-sharing and proportionality in government, but has added the capacity for smaller qualifying parties under d'Hondt to eschew membership of the Executive and play a formal role in opposition. Importantly, the PfG was agreed upon quite quickly by the DUP and Sinn Fein after the May 2016 Assembly Election when it was a bilateral discussion, avoiding the long periods of inter-party wrangling between members of the five-party Grand Coalition that had plagued previous mandates. It all went wrong after that, with another election forced eight months later and no restoration of devolution in sight at the time of writing (November 2017) – but this does not take away from the internal coherence of the mechanics of the system. It instead highlights the incapacity of those operating it.

Modelling mechanisms for political reform

In addition to a non-statutory move towards a formal opposition, certain informal changes may help the political institutions adapt in a way that promotes rather than further jeopardises their stability. Some of these are underway. For instance, converting the Office of First and Deputy First Minister (OFMDFM) into the Executive was a consequence of the Fresh Start Agreement and was introduced at the beginning of the May 2016 parliamentary mandate following the assembly election. This does not materially affect the distribution of power connected to these posts, as both are co-equal in practice. It should, however, help to convey the sense of unity of purpose in the Executive, rather than defining it as a binary post between opposing ethnonational blocs. While the positions of First and Deputy First Minister remained within the newly coined Executive Office in 2016, the intention was to affirm partnership between the two largest ethnonational parties and the need to capture the First Minister position in subsequent elections. There is little evidence that this largely symbolic change from OFMDFM to Executive Office has reduced the angst over this issue (especially in the DUP and its support base) though this may in part be due to the fact that it suits the DUP to keep the issue alive. The party has fought the last several elections with the core message to unionist voters that the only way to keep SF out of the First Minister role is to vote for the DUP.

Alternatively, the largest political parties of each designation could form a coalition government automatically (as informally agreed and implemented in the post-Ohrid Republic of Macedonia), enabling their smaller intra-ethnic competitors to form an effective opposition (Koneska 2012). These options might become more attractive if the United Kingdom becomes more decentralised in the aftermath of Brexit and if Scotland follows through with independence, assuming there is another referendum on the issue after the UK leaves the EU.

So far, an option missing from the Northern Ireland power-sharing model is the ability to form a government under a pre-agreed coalition programme, with majorities on both sides of the divide as, for instance, in Belgium, admittedly not an unproblematic option (as discussed elsewhere in this volume) The Northern Ireland experience to this point is that the assembly has many oppositional voices but they are *ad hoc* and piecemeal, sometimes becoming platforms for personality politics rather than the presentation of alternative programmes for government. As McCrudden et al. (2016) argue, it is important to stress that the broadly inclusive d'Hondt mechanism should remain a default option if other possibilities are not negotiated following elections. In fact, as discussed at length in Chapter 3, the absence of formal d'Hondt-style arrangements has left countries in similar situations without elected governments for prolonged periods, as in Belgium in 2010 and 2011. The Brussels Capital Region uses a spare two-tier system, allowing its Executive to be appointed by political parties, as in Northern Ireland, but only after failing to form a cross-community coalition.

It needs to be recognised that the introduction of more competitive politics in Northern Ireland should be carefully timed and negotiated with the support of all major political parties. Exclusive coalitions could increase uncertainty and rivalry among groups as suggested by Lebanon, Iraq or the former Yugoslavia, where groups have responded violently to attempts by others to ostracise them politically following negotiations to form a government. However, if parties come to see coalitions as equally attractive, there would be no fear of political ostracism. These examples also point to a broader theme in consociational theory and practice, demonstrating how the micro-design of formal and informal institutions can be important in renegotiating new structures in Northern Ireland and potentially other divided societies.

The exogenous challenge: The impact of Brexit on power-sharing in Northern Ireland

The political institutions in Northern Ireland were capable of faltering on their own without the Brexit process – but it does complicate the internal dynamics of power-sharing and does not help establish common ground between the DUP (which supports Brexit) and SF (which opposes it). The result of the June 2016 referendum provided a structural basis for the DUP and Sinn Fein to rationalise their adversarial behaviour. A programme for government, hammered out at great pains following the May 2016 Assembly Election, just a month before the referendum vote, was significantly derailed by the fact that the DUP and Sinn Féin adopted opposing positions on the Brexit issue. The subsequent months further calcified their positions – and this looks likely to become more entrenched as the negotiations take shape during the remainder of 2017 and over the next 18 months, sharpened by the deal struck between the DUP and the Conservative Party after the 8 June 2017 UK General Election. Disagreement over leaving the EU and terms of a post-Brexit deal for Northern Ireland (and the whole island of Ireland), has re-energised an aspect of the NI conflict that many had thought was at least anaesthetised by the GFA in 1998. Since then, the border between Ireland and Northern Ireland has become more of a porous membrane. Now the land border may need to be more formally demarcated and policed, since one side will remain in the EU and the other will be leaving. The Brexit process has also rekindled the Sinn Fein argument that the UK is a malign influence and is interfering negatively in Ireland (see below). The UK General Election on 8 June 2017 and subsequent political arrangement between the British government and DUP has fed the nationalist critique that the peace process and NI are secondary to narrow party political interests in Britain.

In terms of the big picture, there are at least two key areas of concern in relation to how Brexit may affect the power-sharing institutions in Northern Ireland. The first relates to the *process* itself and the uncertainty and ambiguity associated with that across political, economic and cultural stakeholder groups and the broader electorate. As former Irish Ambassador to Great Britain Daniel Mulhall commented, in evidence given to the House of Commons Northern Ireland Affairs Committee on 8 February 2017, 'Nobody can say how these negotiations will end up'.[15] The second zone of concern is related to the policy *outcomes* of Brexit and in particular, to the difficulty of maintaining the Common Travel Area (CTA) in Ireland alongside the UK's declared intention to withdraw from the Customs Union and the Single Market. Both of these aspects have the potential to, separately or in combination, further complicate the process of restoring and operating the devolved institutions in Northern Ireland. Prime Minister Theresa May's off-the-cuff remark in December 2016 that what she really wanted was 'a red white and blue Brexit',[16] demonstrated a lack of understanding (or interest) in how this would be received by ultra-sensitive and highly tuned Northern Ireland hearing. This phrase meant a lot to both nationalists and unionists (for different reasons) and clarified in some minds that the process of the UK leaving the EU would revive the 'constitutional question' in Northern Ireland that was parked (rather than resolved) by the Good Friday Agreement in 1998.

Northern Ireland represents a unique aspect of the Brexit implementation puzzle for the process of leaving the EU, not faced elsewhere in the UK. In short, it will become the frontier to the EU and the only territorial border between the UK and an EU member state. This has potentially huge implications for power-sharing in Northern Ireland – where the border was for many years the physical and legal manifestation of partition and a key driver of violent political conflict between the late 1960s and late 1990s, until the consociational political institutions were established in the wake of the 1998 GFA.

Some politicians, such as former leader of the SDLP Mark Durkan, have already claimed that the Brexit process potentially tears at the legal fabric of the peace process and its political engineering, as defined through the GFA in 1998.[17] In addition, the ratification of the GFA through parallel referendums in Northern Ireland and the Irish Republic in May 1998 was an important exercise of Irish self-determination, which Brexit potentially disrupts by re-emphasising the sovereignty of the UK. Brexit is thus likely to put the 'consent principle' under considerable strain (Phinnemore, 2016; Hayward, Komarova & Buttazzoni, 2016). During the multi-party negotiations that led to the GFA in 1998, the main cause for concern related to the lack of *internal* consensus and legitimacy for the agreement that was reached and the political institutions that eventually followed – few foresaw the sort of *external* complications to this system that the Brexit decision has produced. There is an argument to be made, therefore, that it undermines the dual referenda process that ratified the GFA document in 1998, as the removal of NI from the EU and the removal of UK legal obligations to the EU that were written into the GFA alters the basis upon which voters in both parts of Ireland cast their ballots in those referenda in 1998. While this may be regarded as a pedantic point in the greater scheme of Brexit challenges that will be faced over the next two years and beyond, it does not reduce the prospect that it will become a point of contention in NI politics and between Ireland and the UK.

Brexit therefore presents a new and unforeseen challenge for power-sharing in Northern Ireland and the broader peace process that was not envisaged by those who negotiated and designed the political system in 1998 or those who further adapted it in subsequent political agreements. The political system that was established in 1998 and 1999 incorporated commitments that the UK cannot easily withdraw from without affecting the GFA and the Republic of Ireland – which revised its own constitution following a referendum in 1998 based, in part, on these commitments. Leaving aside the unknown economic impacts, a hard Brexit threatens to emphasise the Britishness and Irishness of the two jurisdictions, shining a harsh, unforgiving light on the 'constitutional question'. The manifestation of a 'hard' border in Ireland will make explicit what has been implicit since the peace process, namely the binary nature of political sovereignty. The Britishness of Northern Ireland and the Irishness of the Republic will become a more starkly evident binary choice and the post-GFA fuzziness over political identity and citizenship will become more difficult to sustain. This 'constructive ambiguity' has arguably been part of the glue that has held the power-sharing system together since its emergence from the GFA in 1999. Neither unionists nor nationalists were faced with a constitutional fait accompli – they were allowed to hold diametrically opposite objectives, while co-operating on day-to-day political and economic priorities.

Recent survey evidence suggests that once we break down the 56% "Remain" vote in the 23 June Brexit referendum, we find that 85% of Catholic/nationalist voters supported Remain, while only 38% of Protestant/unionist voters did likewise.[18] This maps on quite starkly across the party political spectrum also, with majorities for "Leave" in the two largest unionist parties, DUP (70%) and UUP (54%), and overwhelming majorities for Remain in the two largest nationalist parties, SF (86%) and SDLP (92%).[19] This underscores the above point that Brexit represents a structural barrier, rather than a point of commonality, between unionist and nationalist political parties and their respective electoral bases in Northern Ireland. It aligns with, rather than complicates, the ethnonational division within Northern Ireland. Thus it further problematises the notion that unionist and nationalist political representatives will be able to establish a basis for sharing power on a common policy platform in the future.

Conclusion

The argument here has been that consociational power-sharing in Northern Ireland is the correct political system to pursue but that adaptations are needed to provide it with greater flex and reflexivity in response to the changing local context.

The point is to highlight that the power-sharing system is evolving beyond the initial conceptual boundaries of the consociational model envisaged in 1998 and that possibilities now exist to strengthen and build upon what has already been delivered. Arguing for targeted informal changes in the political system neither undervalues its benefits nor undermines the credibility of the consociational structures that have delivered them. In other words, there is room for manoeuvring between binary positions. Some scholars have pointed out that the political system in Northern Ireland represents 'a dramatic success story' (McCrudden, et al., 2016); others have claimed that its consociational structure dooms it to sectarian apartheid, endemic weakness and enduring division (Horowitz, 2002; Taylor, 2009; Wilford & Wilson, 2001). We see an informal space existing between these two positions that could be further expanded to build a more adaptable, durable and responsive form of consociationalism in Northern Ireland – and elsewhere.

As we outline in the other two chapters of the book, there is capacity to move beyond the consociational/centripetal dichotomy and develop power-sharing that draws on the advantages of both. To critique the failures of the devolved government (to move substantially away from conflict management/accommodationist policies) is not to attack the consociational fabric of the post-GFA institutions. It is the obverse. The consociational approach is the correct one for Northern Ireland, but 'coercive consociationalism' in post-conflict societies must evolve from its conflict management accommodationist origins into a transformative space that integrates institutions, political parties and the wider community. This can be achieved while retaining the underpinning elements of cross-community power-sharing and proportionality that lie at the heart of the power-sharing model in Northern Ireland.

The movement from *government without opposition* towards *government with opposition(s)*, from 2007 to 17, demonstrates the capacity of consociationalism to evolve via a combination of formal and informal agreements between the political parties. As the next chapter suggests, power-sharing settlements cannot be static, and Northern Ireland could move in the direction of 'living consociationalism' as suggested in our next chapter, on Brussels. A more dynamic view on power-sharing also holds out the realistic prospect of the next mandate in Northern Ireland expanding to include effective policy delivery once the DUP and SF get to a point where they can agree to restore the power-sharing structures. As explained above, there are both endogenous and exogenous challenges ahead – but they are far from being insurmountable if sufficient political will exists to confront them.

Notes

1 Rt Hon Enoch Powell MP speaking in House of Commons debate 30 June 1978. See Hansard, *HC Deb 30 June 1978 vol 952 1744*, http://hansard.millbank systems.com/commons/1978/jun/30/northern-ireland-government-1
2 Ibid. 1780.
3 The Multi-Party Agreement reached in Northern Ireland in 1998 is variously referred to as the Good Friday Agreement, Belfast Agreement or Belfast/Good Friday Agreement. For the sake of linguistic convenience this book mainly uses Good Friday Agreement and its abbreviated form (GFA).

4 The danger here – which is relevant to other divided societies – is not that Northern Ireland will return to intractable armed conflict, but that sectarian and structural divisions will become further embedded in the political system.

5 Kane, A. 'It's Time to Reject Our Congenital Farce of a Political Process Is Redundant'. *News Letter*, 21 August 2017.

6 McCallister was an independent unionist representing South Down; he left the Ulster Unionist Party in 2013 and went on to form the ill-fated Northern Ireland 21 (NI21). This imploded shortly after it was formed with allegations of misconduct made against party leader Basil McCrea. McCallister left NI21 and continued as an independent unionist. He lost his seat in the 2016 Assembly Election and did not stand for election in 2017. He was appointed to the Northern Ireland Human Rights Commission in August 2017.

7 Formally introduced on 23 September 2015 and known as the Assembly and Executive Reform (Assembly Opposition) Bill (NIA 62/11–16). For detailed information on the passage of the bill through the assembly, see Report into the Assembly & Executive Reform (Assembly Opposition) Bill, Eighth Report February 2016.

8 Under the terms of the GFA and current rules of the devolved institutions, all elected MLAs have to designate themselves as being 'nationalist' or 'unionist' when registering as an MLA on the first day the assembly meets after an election. The purpose of this procedure is to facilitate cross-community voting within the assembly. MLAs who refuse to choose one of these two categories are defined as 'others' within the system.

9 See www.legislation.gov.uk/nia/2016/10/contents

10 SDLP. Eastwood's Leader Address to #SDLP16. 31 March 2016 https://www.sdlp.ie/ga/news/2016/colum-eastwoods-leader-address-to-sdlp16/

11 www.theyworkforyou.com/ni/?id=2016-02-29.7.23&s=speaker%3A13811

12 www.irishnews.com/news/2017/08/31/news/lord-kilclooney-says-nationalists-are-not-equal-to-unionists-1124541

13 www.bbc.co.uk/news/uk-northern-ireland-41111823

14 http://www.newsletter.co.uk/news/late-move-sees-sdlp-join-sf-to-veto-parts-of-opposition-bill-1-7194418
Securing Wales' Future, Published by the Welsh Government. January 2017 https://beta.gov.wales/sites/default/files/2017-01/30683%20Securing%20Wales%C2%B9%20Future_ENGLISH_WEB.pdf

15 Walker, S. 'Brexit: Irish Border Crossings "Impossible to Monitor"' BBC News, 7 February 2017, www.bbc.co.uk/news/uk-northern-ireland-politics-38907472

16 www.bbc.co.uk/news/38223990

17 https://hansard.parliament.uk/commons/2016-12-07/debates/CA09D9B2-9634-41C8-8979-8B9CD82DBB8F/TheGovernmentSPlanForBrexit

18 Garry, John ESRC NI Assembly Election Study (2016)

19 Ibid.

Bibliography

Assembly and Executive Reform Act 2016 www.legislation.gov.uk/nia/2016/10/contents

BBC News (2016) 'SDLP's Colum Eastwood not concerned about party being squeezed in DUP and Sinn Féin battle.' 12 March. See www.bbc.co.uk/news/uk-northern-ireland-politics-35788345 (Last accessed 30 March 2016)

Cochrane, F. (2012) 'From Transition to Transformation in Ethnonational Conflict: Some Lessons from Northern Ireland.' *Ethnopolitics* 11 (2): 182–203.

Cochrane, F. (2013a) 'Assembly and Executive Review Committee Stakeholder "Call for Evidence" Paper on Review of D'Hondt Community Designation and Provisions for Opposition', *Review of D'Hondt, Community Designation and Provisions for Opposition, Assembly and Executive Review Committee Report*: NIA 123/11–15, 18 June, pp. 207–15. Available at www.niassembly.gov.uk/Documents/Reports/Assem_Exec_Review/nia-123-11-15-Review-of-DHondt-Community-Designation-and-Provisions-for-Opposition.PDF

Cochrane, F. (2013b) *Northern Ireland: The Reluctant Peace*, London & New Haven: Yale University Press.

Fresh Start Agreement. (2015) http://cain.ulst.ac.uk/events/peace/stormont-agreement/Stormont_Agreement_2015-11-17.pdf

Gilligan, C. (2008) 'Northern Ireland Ten Years After the Agreement.' *Ethnopolitics* 7 (1): 1–19.

Hayward, K., Komarova, M., & Buttazzoni, M. (2016) *Brexit and the Border: Managing the UK/Ireland Impact*. Queen's University Belfast. https://pure.qub.ac.uk/portal/files/123024606/Brexit_and_the_UK_Ireland_Border_Discussion_Paper.pdf

Horowitz, D. (1993) 'The Challenge of Ethnic Conflict: Democracy in Divided Societies.' *Journal of Democracy* 4 (4): 18–38.

Horowitz, D. (2002) 'Explaining the Northern Ireland Agreement: The Sources of an Unlikely Constitutional Consensus.' *British Journal of Political Science* 32 (2): 193–220.

Koneska, C. (2012). *Between Accommodation and Resistance: Political Elites in Post-Conflict Bosnia and Macedonia*, PhD Thesis, University of Oxford, St Antony's College.

Lijphart, A. (1977) *Democracy in Plural Societies: A Comparative Exploration*, New Haven: Yale University Press.

Lijphart, A. (2004) 'Constitutional Design for Divided Societies.' *Journal of Democracy* 15 (2): 96–109.

Loizides, N. (2016) *Designing Peace: Cyprus and Institutional Innovation in Divided Societies*, University of Pennsylvania Press, Philadelphia, PA.

McCrudden, C., McGarry, J., O'Leary, B., & Schwartz, A. (2013) 'Memorandum for the Northern Ireland Assembly and Executive Review Committee', *Review of D'Hondt, Community Designation and Provisions for Opposition, Assembly and Executive Review Committee Report*: NIA 123/11–15, 18 June, pp. 228–38. Available at: www.niassembly.gov.uk/Documents/Reports/Assem_Exec_Review/nia-123-11-15-Review-of-DHondt-Community-Designation-and-Provisions-for-Opposition.PDF

McCrudden, C., McGarry, J., O'Leary, B., & Schwartz, A. (2016) 'Why Northern Ireland's Institutions Need Stability' *Government and Opposition* 51 (1): 30–58.

McCulloch, A. (2013) 'Does Moderation Pay? Centripetalism in deeply Divided Societies.' *Ethnopolitics* 12 (2): 111–132.

McEvoy, J. (2014) 'The Role of External Actors in Incentivizing Post-Conflict Power-Sharing.' *Government and Opposition* 49(1), 47–69.

McEvoy, J. (2015). *Power-Sharing Executives: Governing in Bosnia, Macedonia, and Northern Ireland.* National and Ethnic Conflict in the 21st Century, University of Pennsylvania Press, Philadelphia, PA.

McGarry, J. (Ed.). (2001) *Northern Ireland and the Divided World*, Oxford: Oxford University Press.

McGarry, J., & Loizides N. (2015) 'Power-Sharing in a Re-United Cyprus: Centripetal Coalitions vs. Proportional Sequential Coalitions.' *International Journal of Constitutional Law* 13 (4): 847–872.

McGarry, J., & O'Leary, B. (2004) *The Northern Ireland Conflict: Consociational Engagements*, Oxford University Press, Oxford.

McGarry, J., & O'Leary, B. (2006) 'Consociational Theory, Northern Ireland's Conflict, and its Agreement. Part 2: What Critics of Consociation can Learn from Northern Ireland.' *Government and Opposition* 41 (2): 249–277.

Mitchell, P. (2001) 'Transcending an Ethnic Party System: The Impacts of Consociational Governance on Electoral Dynamics and the Party System' in R. Wilford (ed.) *Aspects of the Belfast Agreement*, Oxford University Press, Oxford, pp. 28–48.

Nolan, P. (2014) *Northern Ireland Peace Monitoring Report* (Number Three), Community Relations Council, March, Belfast.

Northern Ireland Assembly Review Committee. (2013) *Review of d'Hondt, Community Designation and Provisions for Opposition.* http://www.niassembly.gov.uk/globalassets/Documents/Reports/Assem_Exec_Review/nia-123-11-15-Review-of-DHondt-Community-Designation-and-Provisions-for-Opposition.PDF

O'Leary, B. (1989) 'The Limits to Coercive Consociationalism in Northern Ireland.' *Political Studies* 37 (4): 562–588.

Phinnemore, D. (2016) 'Northern Ireland and Brexit: Limits and Opportunities for a New Relationship with the EU' *Northern Ireland Assembly Knowledge Exchange Series 2016–2017.* 12 October. https://qub.ac.uk/brexit/Brexitfilestore/Filetoupload,728117,en.pdf

Reilly, B. (2012) 'Institutional Designs for Diverse Democracies: Consociationalism, Centripetalism and Communalism Compared.' *European Political Science* 11 (2): 259–270.

Robinson, P. (2014) 'Stormont's inadequate set-up and the welfare row . . . Northern Ireland's First Minister writes exclusively for the Telegraph.' *Belfast Telegraph*, 9 September 2014. Available at: www.belfasttelegraph.co.uk/debateni/blogs/stormonts-inadequate-setup-and-the-welfare-row-northern-irelands-first-minister-writes-exclusively-for-the-telegraph-30570776.html (Last accessed 9 September 2014)

Ruane, J., & Todd, J. (2010) *From "A Shared Future" to "Cohesion Sharing and Integration": An Analysis of Northern Ireland's Policy Framework Documents*, Dublin: IBIS, UCD, October, pp. 1–8.

SDLP Manifesto (2016) *Build A Better Future.* www.sdlp.ie/site/assets/files/43032/sdlp_manifesto_web-1.pdf

Tannam, E. (2012) 'The European Union and Conflict Resolution: Northern Ireland, Cyprus and Bilateral Cooperation.' *Government and Opposition* 47 (1): 49–73.

Taylor, R. (2009) 'The Injustice of a Consociational Solution to the Northern Ireland Problem' in R. Taylor (ed.), *Consociational Theory: McGarry & O'Leary and the Northern Ireland Conflict.* Abingdon: Routledge.

Ulster Unionist Party. (2016) 'Make It Work.' Assembly Election Manifesto. http://uup.org/assets/images/assembly%20manifesto.pdf

Walker, S. (2017) 'Brexit: Irish Border Crossings "Impossible to Monitor".' *BBC News*, 7 February. www.bbc.co.uk/news/uk-northern-ireland-politics-38907472

Whiting, M. (2016) 'Moderation Without Change: The Strategic Transformation of Sinn Féin and the IRA in Northern Ireland.' *Government and Opposition*, early view pp. 1–24. doi: 10.1017/gov.2016.19.

Wilford, R., & Wilson, R. (2001) *A Democratic Design? The Political Style of the Northern Ireland Assembly*. Belfast: Democratic Dialogue.

2 'Living consociationalism' in the Brussels Capital Region

Introduction

Institutional arrangements in deeply divided societies are situational. They address a specific political and sociological situation at a certain moment. These situations are, however, likely to evolve over time. The different groups constituting the divided society may change in relative size. The nature of their political demands often shifts. Their degree of satisfaction with respect to the institutional framework in which they operate might fluctuate. In short, the preferences of community groups in divided societies are subject to a complex and continuously evolving set of political, economic and sociological variables. For these reasons, it seems that consociational arrangements in deeply divided societies are likely to eventually be exposed to demands of adjustment. With this backdrop in mind, this book raises the question of the capacity of institutional arrangements in divided societies to adapt to changing political circumstances.

The previous chapter demonstrated how power-sharing in Northern Ireland has addressed the need for institutional reform with relative success. It has, however, been argued that further institutional adjustments are inevitable in Northern Ireland, which can put the equilibrium between communities at risk. The second chapter focuses on the Brussels Capital Region (BCR). The relevance of the BCR's case lies in the region's elegant combination of flexible procedures for institutional reforms with an extensive set of institutional incentives for cooperation between community groups. These two characteristics have largely contributed to the BCR's remarkable capacity both to adapt to evolving demands raised by its two ethno-linguistic groups and to keep the inter-community tensions at a very low level. In this chapter, we argue that this double achievement makes the BCR a more dynamic form of power-sharing than the model adopted in Northern Ireland. We call this form of power-sharing 'living consociationalism'.

Consociational arrangements are traditionally seen as power-sharing arrangements with direct representation and participation of the main community groups in the administration of public institutions (Hartzell, Hoddie 2003: 320; McCulloch,& McGarry 2017: 1–4). The concept of *living consociationalism* accounts for the need of these arrangements to be evolutionary. In this chapter, we argue that *living consociationalism* in BCR is articulated around institutional mechanisms guaranteeing adaptability and cooperation.

In order to present this argument, we begin with a discussion of some key features of the Belgian institutional framework and of the relation between the two primary community groups at the national level. This broad look helps illustrate the institutional specificities of the BCR. The BCR's institutions are then more specifically discussed in the section that follows. While the analysis of their establishment and the reforms they have undergone highlights their capacity to adapt over time, the description of their current design points to the importance of cooperation mechanisms in Brussels' institutions. In the last section, we argue that the BCR's characteristics of adaptability and cooperation provide an example of *living consociationalism*. Finally, we discuss some institutional challenges which may potentially call for future reform in the BCR.

The Belgian context: tensions between two community groups

Article 1 of the Belgian Constitution provides that Belgium is a federal state composed of communities and regions. It, however, has not always been so. In fact, the federal structure is relatively recent in Belgian history. It is the result of a process that formally began in 1970.

Belgian independence was declared on 4 October 1830. After 15 years of an uneasy union with the United Kingdom of the Netherlands, lasting from 1815 until 1830, the Belgian population revolted and eventually seceded from the Netherlands. The revolution was mainly led by the French-speaking bourgeoisie, who denounced the autocratic regime of King William I in general and philosophical, economic and cultural tensions with the Netherlands in particular. On 7 February 1831 the Belgian Constitution was adopted by the constituent assembly.

Belgium's current institutional structure has largely been shaped by a relatively difficult relation between the nation's two main community groups: the Dutch-speaking group, also called Flemish, that predominantly lives in Flanders (north), and the French-speaking group, essentially located in Wallonia (south). Despite the majority of the population speaking Dutch or one of its related dialects, the country was originally constituted as a French-speaking state in which French was the only official language[1] and where the French-speaking elite would claim a majority of the administrative, economic and military positions.

Since the 1919 Treaty of Versailles and the integration of a German-speaking area into the Belgium territory,[2] three language groups are officially recognised in Belgium. Article 4 of the Belgian Constitution indeed provides that Belgium comprises three mono-linguistic regions – the Dutch-speaking region, the French-speaking region and the German-speaking region – and one bilingual region, the region of Brussels-Capital, where French and Dutch are the two administrative languages.[3]

The repartition of the recognised language groups is relatively straightforward in Belgium. Indeed, besides Brussels, where both language groups cohabit the same territory, each language group lives in a clearly defined and separate area.[4] Note that while the proportion of Dutch speakers to French speakers gives the advantage to the former at the national level – at a ratio of roughly 60% to 40% – their relation is inversed at the BCR level, where Dutch speakers represent a small minority of the population, approximately 15%.

This swift historical and sociological description seems to indicate that Belgium can be considered a deeply divided society. Yet this assertion demands some nuances.

To start, a relative cultural divide does indeed exist in Belgium between the two main community groups. This cultural divide is rooted in and maintained by the use of two different languages. The limited capacity of the population to communicate in the other community's language, and thus the limited access to the other community's culture, goes far to explain the existence of this divide (van Parys, Wauters 2006).[5] Beyond the linguistic dimension, the cultural divide is also grounded on diverging philosophical aspirations in the North and in the South of the country. The Flemish population was historically largely catholic, while the French-speaking one was more inclined to secular ideas. These philosophical peculiarities translated in the political arena, with the socialist and the liberal parties traditionally having the upper hand in Wallonia and the Catholic Party dominating the political landscape in Flanders.[6]

A political divide thus also exists in Belgium, rooted in cultural differences between Flanders and Wallonia. Considering this background, it is noteworthy that the current electoral system at the national level does not transcend the community group logic. Given the delimitation of electoral districts, politicians are indeed elected by members of their ethno-linguistic group. In other words, the electoral approach drives politicians to speak to their in-group members and to adopt positions and address concerns which are often peculiar to their community. The electoral system at the national level therefore stimulates a community logic rather than the search for political convergences across community groups.

The economy is a third variable that demonstrates divisions between both community groups. Key economic indicators, such as the unemployment rate, GDP per capita and external trade performances are telling instances in this case. In 2016, the unemployment rate was 4.9% in Flanders, 10.6% in Wallonia and 16.9% in BCR.[7] In 2015, the GDP per capita was 37,329 euros in Flanders, 26,436 euros in Wallonia and 63,273 euros in Brussels. Regarding external trade, the share of the different regions in 2015 were as follows: 83.1% for Flanders, 14.6% for Wallonia and 2.3% for Brussels.[8] These statistics portray but a few markers of the economic dynamics that have largely advantaged the Dutch-speaking community group over the past 50 years.

Together these cultural, political and economic variables have nourished a range of demands within each language group. These demands stretch from the (further) federalisation of the country to the independence of Flanders and Wallonia, and thus the *de facto* end of Belgium.[9] It is noteworthy that these divides have materialised with a rather low degree of violence in Belgium. The most intense phase of tensions in the history of inter-community relations must be traced back to the 1960s, evidenced by the so-called linguistic legislation issue[10] and the Louvain crisis.[11] In comparison with the Northern Ireland and the Cyprus cases, it is thus important to emphasise that the ethno-linguistic relations in Belgium did not reach high levels of hostility (Hepburn 2004). Therefore, the Belgian case should be seen as a rather peaceful form of a deeply divided society.

Considering Belgium, it is clear the tensions between ethno-linguistic groups have been largely captured by the political institutions. The institutions have indeed managed to integrate important demands of the different ethno-linguistic groups, and in doing so to mitigate hostilities between them. The most visible manifestation of the institutions' capacity to address the community groups' demands lies in Belgium's evolution from a unitary to a federal state, granting a limited autonomy to its entities. This metamorphosis was gradual, beginning in 1970 and undergoing six consecutive institutional reforms.

Towards the end of the 1950s, the long-lasting demand of the Dutch-speaking group for some degree of cultural autonomy was given a new impetus by the urge in southern Belgium to get more control of their own economic policies. The Walloon economy was indeed jeopardised by the massive destruction of its heavy industry during the Second World War, as well as its aging technologies. Wallonia thus pushed for a decentralisation of economic policies, hoping to regain control of the region's socio-economic development. Generally speaking, culture was at the core of the concerns of the Dutch-speaking group, while economics was central to the concerns raised by French speakers. The concordance of the Flemish and the Walloon demands resulted in a common agreement on institutional reforms.

The first reform of the Belgian institutions took place in 1970. It provided for a compromise between the approaches handled by both community groups. The Dutch-speaking group obtained the establishment of language borders, and its request for cultural autonomy was addressed through the creation of three communities: the Flemish community, the French-speaking community and the German-speaking community. In contrast, the demand for economic autonomy raised on the Walloon side was only partly considered.

Indeed, while the 1970 reform included in the Belgian Constitution the article 107 quarter providing for the existence of three regions –the Walloon, the Flemish and the Brussels– the creation and the practical organisation of these regions was not taken up in the 1970 reform.

It is only at the second institutional reform, in 1980, that two regions were *de facto* created: the Flemish and the Walloon regions.[12] As for the Brussels, the community groups could not agree on the modalities of its organisation. Brussels citizens had to wait until the third institutional reform, in 1989, for the creation of the Brussels Capital Region. Three other institutional reforms took place, in 1993, 2001 and in 2011–2012. These reforms largely focused on the transfer of competences from the federal level to the communities and regions.[13]

The six institutional reforms have thus transformed the Belgian unitary state into a federal one through the creation of two types of political entities: communities and regions. In the Belgian context, these two terms should be understood as standing legal terms and not in their traditional sociological and geographical acceptations. Under Belgian constitutional law, a 'region' has a clearly defined territory. It has its own parliament and government, and it oversees specific competences.[14] In turn, a 'community' has its own parliament and government, has specific competences and is in charge of people and institutions belonging to the Dutch-speaking, French-speaking or German-speaking groups.[15] Note that, formally, the federal level is the continuation of the previous national institutions and is in charge of the residual competences.[16]

To better understand the Belgian federal architecture, it helps to see it as a superposition model in which the three communities, the three regions and the federal level are juxtaposed (Figure 2.1). Each level has its own competences. These competences are exclusive, so that, theoretically, no conflict of competences should happen between them.[17] The exclusive competences of the different levels also explain why the parliament of each of these entities can prescribe norms which have all the same legal force.

The development of the Belgian federal structure into a juxtaposition of communities, regions and a federal level is the natural consequence of the original demands of the country's two main community groups. The Dutch-speaking population – spread throughout Flanders and Brussels – wanted to gain control of cultural policies. Therefore, they backed a federalisation of the country along community lines. In turn, the Walloons wanted to be in

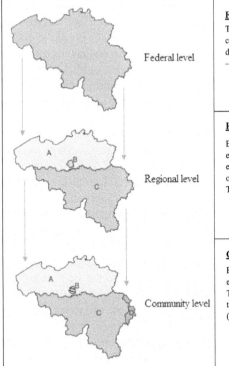

Federal level:
The federal level exercises residual competences–social security, justice, defense, external relations, etc. –over the whole territory.

Regional level:
Each region is in charge of economic, employment, transport, environmental, energy, public work and housing policies on its territory (= territoriality principle). These three regions are:
⇨ Flemish Region (A)
⇨ Brussels Capital Region (B)
⇨ Walloon Region (C)

Community level:
Each community is responsible for health, education and culture policies. These competences are exerted towards individuals and institutions (= individuality principle)
⇨ Flemish Community (A) + (B)
⇨ French-speaking Community (C) + (B)
⇨ German-speaking Community (D)

Figure 2.1 The superposition of the different institutional levels in Belgian federal structure

charge of the economic affairs of their region. However, they did not wish to leave the economic centre of the country, Brussels, to the Dutch-speaking population. Therefore, they pushed for the creation of three regions. The confrontation of the culture-centred communities and the economy-based regions resulted in the establishment of a federal system with several layers, where communities, regions and a federal level are thus intricately linked.

To conclude this first section on a presentation of the broader institutional context in Belgium, one should add that the six institutional reforms did not constitute the progressive implementation of a original master plan. No *a priori* consensus existed between the community groups on the final institutional design to be adopted in Belgium. Reforms were rather taken in order to solve conjunctural political and socio-economic problems that characterised each group.[18] At the centre of these issues lay the status of the bilingual Brussels Capital Region.

The Brussels Capital Region's institutions

The presentation of the Belgian federal structure undertaken in the first section has already highlighted some institutional characteristics of the BCR. Notably, the BCR is the only region of the country where the two main ethno-linguistic groups live together in the same territory. Furthermore, after it was first provided in the Belgian Constitution in 1970, it took almost two decades for the community groups to find an agreement on the organisation of the BCR. The Brussels Capital Region now has its own parliament and government and administers specific competences. Within the relatively sophisticated Belgian federal structure, the BCR institutions should thus be understood both as a constituent region of the federal system and as a microcosm of it, due to the presence of both community groups. While the national ratio of French- to Dutch-speaking populations is roughly 40% to 60%, in Brussels an approximate ratio of 85% to 15% gives the advantage to French speakers.[19] In this context, many of the protective mechanisms guaranteed to the Dutch-speaking community group in BCR mirror those granted to the French-speaking minority at the federal level. The articulation between these two levels certainly contributes to the overall equilibrium between both ethno-linguistic groups in Belgium. We find here some similarities to the Northern Ireland case, where unionists exercise a majority in the North but comprise a significant minority in terms of the whole of Ireland geographically. Nationalists, meanwhile, though a minority in Northern Ireland, represent a sizable majority in terms of the island as a whole. Such numerical distributions carry with them potentially complex assessments of political, economic and cultural interests.

The second section aims to present the BCR institutional model in more details. It begins with an analysis of the establishment and reforms of the regional institutions in Brussels. Then it describes some characteristics of the current institutional design. Overall, this section strives to showcase two things. First, it demonstrates that the repeated revisions of the BCR consociational arrangements illustrate the region's capacity to adapt to evolving socio-political circumstances. Second, it shows that the Brussels institutions have managed to soften the tensions between its French-speaking and Dutch-speaking groups. By doing so, the Brussels institutions have displayed strong faculties in adaptability and cooperation.

The establishment and reforms of the BCR: A case of adaptability

The design of the Brussels institutions has evolved considerably since Belgium moved to federalisation. Their recent development can be segmented into three phases: the first phase spans from the decision to federalise the country in 1970, until the *de facto* creation of the BCR in 1989; the second one ranges from its creation in 1989 until the first substantial reform of its institutions in 2001; and the third phase is from 2001 until the second adaptation of its organisation in 2011–2012.

During the period stretching from the first institutional reform in 1970 until the *de facto* creation of the BCR in 1989, the status of Brussels continuously constituted a major point of disagreement between both community groups. Given the symbolic and economic importance of the Belgian capital, neither could accept leaving Brussels administration to the other. To the Dutch speakers, Brussels stood as an example of the domination of Flemish culture by the French-speaking one. Brussels was indeed a city in which Dutch had been progressively replaced by French as the language of the majority.[20] As such, it was a symbol of the 'Frenchisation' of Flanders which the Dutch-speaking community group was committed to resisting. For this reason, this group pleaded for a co-administration of Brussels by the two communities, or, alternatively, by the federal level. In turn, French speakers were largely in favour of the establishment of Brussels as a third region equal to those of Wallonia and Flanders. They saw this solution as advantageous because, even though Brussels is geographically situated in Flanders, its economic assets would not be appropriated by the Dutch-speaking group.

At the first institutional reform, in 1970, the constitutional assembly proclaimed the existence of three regions. Following the demand of the French-speakers, the article 107 quarter was indeed added to the Belgian Constitution, which provided for the establishment, through a special law, of the Walloon, the Flemish and the Brussels regions. The disagreement between community groups on the organisation and on the functions of the regions in general, and of the BCR in particular, postponed their *de facto* creation.

While the Flemish and the Walloon regions were finally brought into shape at the second institutional reform of 1980, no agreement on the status of Brussels could be found among the community groups. Despite several initiatives in the shape of parliamentary commissions, reflection groups and even the existence of a minister in charge of institutional reforms, it had proven impossible to reach an agreement on the administration of Brussels. The stalemate gave rise to a progressive radicalisation of both community groups (Bruycker 1989: 15).

Nearly a decade into this stalemate, 1988 offered an opportunity for a decisive breakthrough. On 10 May 1988, the new prime minister of Belgium, a Flemish Catholic named Wilfried Maertens,[21] stated in his governmental declaration that his cabinet was about to launch consultations for a third institutional reform. These consultations resulted in an agreement providing for further transfers of competences and finances to the communities and for the establishment of the BCR.[22] Nineteen years after their formal provision in the Constitution, the BCR institutions were finally created. The Special Act of 12 August 1989 on the Brussels Institutions (the 1989 Brussels Act) sets the general principles for the organisation of the BCR.

Article 1 of the 1989 Brussels Act grants the BCR its own parliament and government. The regional parliament is divided in two language groups, the French-speaking Group (FSG) and the Dutch-speaking Group (DSG).[23] The BCR has the same exclusive competences as the Walloon and the Flemish regions. In other words, it is in charge of the economic, employment, transport, environmental, energy, public work and housing policies in its territory.[24] It can adopt its own legal acts around these policies, the ordonnances, which are at the same level in the norm hierarchy as the normal acts passed by the federal and the community assemblies. A French-speaking Community Commission (FsCC), a Flemish Community Commission (FCC) and a Common Community Commission (CCC) are created in Brussels. Their mission is to exert onto the BCR territory some of the competences relating to culture, health and well-being that were traditionally reserved for the communities in the Belgian federal system.[25] The intricate combination of regional institutions with ad hoc community commissions was a compromise between the federalisation logics supported by each community group (Bruycker 1989: 4).

The second phase in the development of the Brussels institutions stretches from the *de facto* creation of the BCR in 1989 until the first substantial reform of its institutions in 2001. Design deficiencies and evolutions within the political landscape in Brussels called for some adjustments to the BCR institutions. While the design deficiencies had to do with the insufficient financing of the FsCC and the overly weak representation of the Dutch-speaking community group within the BCR parliament, the political evolution that called for intervention was related to the worrying growth in Brussels of the *Vlaams Blok*, a Flemish extreme right and nationalist party (Uyttendaele 2002: 202). These various issues eventually led to the reform included in the Lombard agreement of 2001. It is noteworthy that the Lombard agreement was the result of negotiations between Brussels' partners and spillover effects from the federal level.

The federal level indeed deeply influenced the design and conclusion of the 2001 Lombard agreement. After the 1999 legislative elections, the newly elected prime minister of Belgium, the Flemish liberal Guy Verhofstadt, responded to the growing demand of the community groups to initiate a fifth institutional reform by setting up the Intergovernmental and Inter-parliamentary Conference for Institutional Renewal (IICIR). This conference was charged with composing proposals on ways to further adjust the institutional structures in Belgium.

After several weeks of intense negotiations, the IICIR finally presented a document providing, *inter alia*, for the transfer of additional competences from the federal level to the communities and the regions as well as for a refinancing of the communities. These reforms were included in the Lambermont agreement of October 2000 and January 2001. In order to be formally adopted, it remained to the Lambermont agreement to be enacted in a special act by the federal parliament. This required a majority within each language group and two-thirds of the votes overall. The governing majority that championed the reform, however, lacked the two-thirds majority required for the enactment of the agreement. Therefore, they demanded the support of the members of the Volksunie, a Flemish nationalist party from the opposition. The Volksunie only agreed to support the reforms if some of their institutional demands were met at another level, namely at the BCR, where institutional negotiations were also ongoing (Dumont 2002: 28). In other words, the key role that the Volksunie acquired thanks to the special act procedure enabled the Flemish party to tie both negotiations together, which were taking place at the federal level and BCR level, and to gain some bargaining power in the Brussels negotiations (Dumont 2002; Nassaux 2001: 23). Another effect of the Flemish nationalist party was to link the fate of the Lambermont agreement to the success of the negotiations in Brussels. The negotiating parties in Brussels thus became subject to extreme pressures from the federal level (Nassaux 2001: 30). Overall, the spillover effects of the federal level thus materialised in the special position of the Volksunie in the Brussels negotiations, and in the tremendous pressures exerted by the federal government to reach an agreement. These observations show how the federal level influenced the proceedings of the negotiations between the Brussels partners for the conclusion of the 2001 Lombard agreement. Now what exactly did the Brussels negotiators agree upon?

The negotiations taking place at the BCR level had several objectives. They aimed to smooth the interplay between both community groups in the capital; find a way to address the chronic lack of finances for the FsCC; provide for a stronger representation of the DSG within the BCR parliament;[26] and find an institutional answer to potential problems linked to the growing importance of the Vlaams Blok in the DSG. A working group was established for the BCR negotiations. This working group had a mandate to draft solution proposals to the Brussels institutional problems.[27] These proposals resulted in the adoption of the following measures.

In Brussels, the weak representation of the DSG in the BCR parliament, combined with their required participation in parliamentary commissions, meant the deputies of the DSG were literally overloaded with work (Nassaux 2000: 13).[28] In order to address this problem, the Dutch-speaking community group asked for a larger representation within the assembly. They obtained an increase in the number of seats from 75 to 89, 17 of which were secured to the DSG while the FSG received the remaining 72 seats. Guaranteed representation of the DSG was a key demand that the Volksunie could impose thanks to its special position at the negotiation table.

A second issue that stood at the core of the negotiation agenda was the growing weight of the Vlaams Blok in the DSG in Brussels. The increasing number of seats they had obtained in past legislatures threatened a paralysis of the BCR institutions for proceedings requiring a double majority – ordonnances requiring a majority in each language group and in the parliament overall – as well as acts taken by the CCC (Uyttendaele 2014: 181).[29] Hence, a procedure as fundamental as the election of the BCR ministers by the parliament, which normally requires a double majority, was put at severe risk given the ideological opposition between the democratic parties and the Vlaams Blok. In order to address this issue, the negotiators agreed on a technical emergency proceeding in case of institutional paralysis. This procedure provides for transferring the vote to the FCC, which comprises the members of the DSG plus five members from the Flemish parliament. These five additional members should make it possible for the democratic parties to get the majority and to overcome the issue represented by the Vlaams Blok.

Overall, the risk posed by the far right in Brussels, as well as the concomitant existence of specific demands on each side – the pronounced need of the French speakers to refinance the FsCC and the guaranteed representation asked for by the Dutch speakers – enabled both linguistic groups to go beyond their divisions and to reach an agreement in Brussels. The Lombard agreement was signed on 29 April 2001.[30]

As had been the case for the Lambermont agreement, it appeared that the Lombard agreement could not gather the majority it needed to be adopted in a special act by the federal parliament. More specifically, the agreement did not obtain a majority in the French-speaking group of the federal assemblies. In order to reach this majority, the French-speaking parties championing the Lombard agreement approached the PSC, the French-speaking Catholic party. In exchange for the abstention of the latter during the vote, the former accepted some of their demands on a re-financing of education. A compromise on this specific issue was thus reached between French speakers in the Saint Boniface agreement, and the enactment of both the Lombard and the Lambermont agreements was saved. Together the Lambermont agreement, the Lombard agreement and the Saint Boniface agreement represent a subtle balance (Delwit, Hellings 2001: 43, 50).

The third key phase analysed in this discussion of the development of the BCR institutions stretched from 2001 until the second reform of the BCR institutions, which were held at the sixth state reform in 2011–2012.

The agreement on the sixth state reform was reached on 11 October 2011 after 541 days of institutional crisis in Belgium. This agreement brought an end to the longest political stalemate in Belgian history. It is made up of several sub-agreements, some of which concern the organisation, the functioning and the financing of the Brussels institutions. Overall, it should be said that the 2011–2012 reform did not entail many fundamental changes to the BCR. It is most important to note that, besides the transfer of new competences to the regions, Brussels was also granted constitutive autonomy and a 'Brussels community' was created.

The label 'Brussels community' might be confusing in the Belgian federal context. This institution has indeed nothing to do with the traditional understanding of the term 'community'. Instead, it is a cooperation and consultation body that brings public authorities together – amongst which are the three regions, the federal authority, and others – to discuss the practical implementation of regional competences that affect the socio-economic interests of Brussels.[31] It is thus aimed at finding coordinated solutions to practical issues, like accessing the capital by public transportation or by car. The sixth institutional reform also grants a limited constitutive autonomy to the BCR. From then on, the BCR institutions have the capacity to decide on some of their organisational and functioning rules. This capacity is thus no longer exclusively under the competence of the federal legislator. Finally, new competences such as tourism, family allocations and the like were also transferred to the regional level.[32]

Since they were first enacted in 1989, institutional arrangements in the BCR thus have been the object of two substantial revisions in 2001 and in 2011–2012. A key dimension of the BCR's capacity to adapt over time is certainly the legal framework regulating the procedure for the adoption of these arrangements. In Brussels, these proceeding rules have indeed displayed a subtle mix of flexibility and rigidity. What, then, are the characteristics of these rules?

Generally, one considers that the enactment of a political agreement on the Brussels institutional structure can occur in three types of legal instruments: in the Belgian Constitution, in a special act adopted by the federal parliament and in a special ordonnance adopted by the BCR parliament. The procedures for these three types of enactment are different.

Regarding a constitutional enactment, article 195 of the Belgian Constitution sets the procedure by which the revision of the Constitution has to proceed. It states:

> The federal legislative power has the right to declare that there are reasons to revise such constitutional provision as it determines. Following such a declaration, the two Houses are automatically dissolved. Two

new Houses are then convened, in accordance with Article 46. These Houses make decisions, in common accord with the King, on the points submitted for revision. In this case, the Houses can only debate provided that at least two thirds of the members who make up each House are present; and no change is adopted unless it is supported by at least two thirds of the votes cast.

(Belgian Constitution, Article 195)

Under article 195 of the Constitution, the federal parliament is the only institution allowed to revise the basic law. If it wants to proceed to such revision, it first needs to indicate which provisions of the Constitution it intends to revise. This decision must be taken by a majority of the parliament's members within both houses and with respect to the same list of provisions. After having reached an agreement on the provisions that should be open for revision and after this agreement has been supported by a majority in both houses, the parliament is then dissolved and new elections are organised. The newly elected houses are free to revise (or not) the provisions mentioned in the revision list. However, they are bound by this list in the sense that they cannot revise provisions other than those indicated in the list. For a provision to be revised, two-thirds of the members of each house must vote for it, provided that at least two-thirds of its members are taking part in the vote. Overall, this procedure is extremely demanding as it entails the dissolution of the parliament, the organisation of new elections, a two-thirds quorum and a two-thirds majority in both houses.

In order to slightly ease the proceedings for the adoption of institutional reforms, the constituent power has established an alternative procedure, the adoption of 'special acts'.

When negotiating the constitutional reform of 1970, the community groups did not manage to reach an agreement on the specific design of the regions. Indeed, they could not reach the two-thirds majority necessary for constitutional reforms. However, they took care to include in the basic law a provision establishing a specific procedure for the creation and the organisation of regions in Belgium, article 107 quarter ancient. This article was broken down into two articles at the 1993 re-coordination of the Constitution, the new articles 3 and article 39 of the Constitution. While article 3 enounces the creation of three regions, article 39 deals with the legal procedure for the *de facto* establishment of these regions. It reads:

The law assigns to the regional bodies that it creates and that are composed of elected representatives the power to manage the matters that it determines, with the exception of those referred to in Articles 30 and 127 to 129, within the scope and according to the manner laid down by a law. This law must be passed by a majority as described in Article 4, last paragraph.

(Belgian Constitution, Article 39)

Article 39 of the Constitution provides that regional bodies are created by law and that such law determines the matters which are the responsibility of the regions. It adds that this law must be adopted with the special majority defined in article 4 of the Constitution. In turn, article 4's last paragraph states that,

> The boundaries of the four linguistic regions can only be changed or corrected by a law passed by a majority of the votes cast in each linguistic group in each House, on condition that a majority of the members of each group is present and provided that the total number of votes in favour that are cast in the two linguistic groups is equal to at least two thirds of the votes cast.

(Belgian Constitution, Article 4)

Article 4 of the Constitution thus sets four conditions for the adoption of a special act. To begin with, it fixes a participation quorum of minimum 50% plus one in each language group. Then, the act needs to be supported by a majority of the expressed votes in each language group. Besides this minimum support, the act also has to be backed by at least two-thirds of the voters, regardless of their linguistic affiliation. Finally, this procedure has to take place in both houses of the federal parliament. Agreements adopted through a special act must, of course, respect the constitutional provisions, which are, in the Belgian legal system, of a higher rank. The special legislator is thus bound by the principles set up in the Constitution.

The special act of 12 August 1989 on the Brussels Institutions has thus been adopted according to the procedure provided in article 4 of the Belgian Constitution. It is noteworthy that, in the Belgian federal system, decisions on *the design of the BCR institutions* have to be enacted within the *federal* parliament. This subordination of the organisational and functioning rules of the BCR institutions to the federal level confirms that the question of the status of Brussels goes beyond its own population and indeed that the BCR remains a sensitive issue for which both community groups in their whole have to be consulted. This subordination has, however, been slightly softened at the sixth state's reform in 2011–2012.

Unlike in many other federal states, the federal entities in Belgium cannot adopt their own constitution. They do, however, benefit from a certain 'constitutive autonomy' –a capacity to decide for themselves their organisational and procedural rules.[33] The constitutive autonomy granted to the BCR is limited in two aspects. First, the BCR cannot decide on the competences it wants to exert.[34] Second, with respect to its organisational and procedural rules, the BCR can only decide on some aspects, such as how the parliament sessions are organised, whether or not they are public or whether or not the government should attend the sessions. The BCR can also fix the duration of the legislature, the day of the election, the procedural rules for the government and the status of its members, the number of ministers provided that besides the minister-president the parity is respected and so on.[35] However, the BCR *cannot* decide on the number of seats in the parliament, how the seats are allocated between language groups nor the number of ministers coming from each language group. Nor can it change the collegiality and consensus rules within the government, the alarm bell procedure and other such things. In other words, a constitutive autonomy has been granted by the federal level to the BCR for matters which do not directly relate to the inter-community groups' relations. Indeed, the rules affecting the overall equilibrium between both community groups, at the center of which one finds the rules on the protection of the Dutch-speaking minority in Brussels, remain under the competences of the special federal legislator.

From the sixth institutional reform onwards, the BCR has thus been granted the capacity to bring some modifications to its institutions by special ordonnances. In turn, these ordonnances need to follow a special procedure in order to be adopted. This procedure requires a special majority – a majority within each language group and a two-thirds majority in the whole parliament.[36] Hence, the decisions on how the BCR organises and how it functions are taken, no longer exclusively at the federal level, but also by the Brussels institutions themselves (Uyttendaele 2014). In that sense, the limited constitutive autonomy granted to the BCR can be understood as the beginning of the emancipation of the Brussels institutions from their subordination to the federal level and thus, as the first move towards a possible decoupling of the community group relations in Brussels from those at the federal level.

To sum up, there are a set of three possible legal procedures for institutional reforms in the BCR: a reform of the BCR can happen through a revision of the Constitution, through the adoption of a special act or through the vote of a special ordonnance. It is noteworthy that each of these three procedures addresses different types of organisational and functioning rules. While the Belgian Constitution limits itself to a definition of the general principles and characteristics of the federal system – for instance, it just enounces the existence of three regions[37] – the special acts organise the concrete implementation of the general framework set in the constitution. Finally, the special ordonnances deal with matters less essential to the community groups' relation in Brussels. Accordingly, the procedure for the adoption of each of these legal instruments has a different degree of stringency. Article 195 of the Belgian Constitution sets up a procedure that implies an *a priori* agreement on the provisions open for revision. It implies a dissolution of the parliament and the organisation of new parliamentary elections, and it requires a two-thirds majority. In turn, a special act necessitates a majority within both language groups of the federal parliament and a two-thirds majority overall. Finally, a special ordonnance is adopted thanks to a simple majority in each language group of the BCR parliament and a two-thirds majority in the parliament as a whole.

While the idea of the creation of regions was enacted in the Belgian Constitution in 1970 according to the procedure provided under article 195 of the Constitution, the BCR was established by the 1989 Brussels Act, adopted in accordance with the procedure inherent to special acts provided under article 4 of the Constitution. The 1989 Brussels Act underwent about 15 revisions, both major and minor, until 2015. The major revisions were those adopted at the institutional reforms of 2001 and 2011–2012, as discussed in section 2. All 15 reforms were approved by the federal parliament according to the special act procedure. However, for the first time, in 2015, the 1989 Brussels Act was amended not by a special act but by a special ordonnance of the BCR parliament.[38] The constitutional revisions, the special acts and the special ordonnances are thus the legal instruments by which the BCR's institutions have taken shape and have gradually been modified. They are the legal mechanisms by which the BCR has been able to adapt to changing political, economic and sociological circumstances.

Overall, the design of the BCR institutions has evolved considerably over the past decades. The previous paragraphs sketched some of the most important features of these evolutions and illustrated the subtle mix of flexibility and rigidity displayed by the legal procedures for the enactment of these reforms. More specifically, we have seen that problems related to growth of the Vlaams Blok, the need for refinancing the FsCC, the wish to improve the coordination of socio-economic policies in the BCR, the demand of the DSG for guaranteed representation and the willingness to acquire constitutive autonomy were all factors which influenced inter-community group relations in the BCR. In other words, political issues, economic demands and sociological evolutions called for a gradual adaptation of the institutional structure in Brussels. This analysis of the establishment and the reforms of the BCR institutions showcase the capacity of the BCR institutions to adapt over time. The next paragraphs are dedicated to describing the current institutional structure of the BCR. This description highlights another key characteristic of the BCR, namely its implementation of cooperation mechanisms.

The current institutional structure of the BCR:
a case of cooperation

The several reforms of the BCR resulted in a rather sophisticated institutional architecture. This institutional architecture can be seen as a two-sided coin. On one side, it provides for strong protection mechanisms for the Dutch-speaking minority in Brussels. In turn, these protection mechanisms require a high degree of cooperation between the parties in order to avoid any institutional stalemate. This emphasis on cooperation represents the other side of the coin. Mechanisms protecting the Dutch-speaking community, and thus calling for inter-group cooperation in the BCR, are presented in the next paragraphs.

Given the bilingual status of Brussels, the parliament has been organized from its creation into two language groups. Each political party running for the regional elections in Brussels must therefore be registered in the FSG or in the DSG. A list cannot be registered in both groups. Let us note that this system owes some similarity to the community designation function for members elected to the assembly in Northern Ireland. On election day voters can decide whether they want to vote for candidates belonging to the French-speaking or the Dutch-speaking lists (Coffé 2006, 100). In a region where citizens have a more or less acute sense of belonging to a language group, and considering that group identities may or may not be fixed for voters,[39] it was thought inappropriate to lock them into a group. Article 23 of the 1989 Brussels Act specifies that members elected from Dutch-speaking lists constitute the DSG, whereas members elected from French-speaking lists constitute the FSG in the BCR parliament. The parliament consists of 89 seats, with the FSG automatically receiving 72 seats and the DSG being allocated 17 seats. Its members are elected for a period of five years.

Besides this guaranteed representation, the Dutch-speaking minority benefits from other protection mechanisms within the BCR parliament (Bodson, Loizides 2017). Most important among these mechanisms are the double majority rule and the 'alarm bell' procedure. The double majority rule implies that for certain matters a double majority – that is, a majority in the whole parliament plus a majority within each language group – is required to adopt a draft of law.[40] In turn, the 'alarm bell' procedure provides that when three-quarters of the members of a language group consider that a draft of law threatens the relationship between both communities in Brussels, they can trigger an *alarm bell*.[41] This will suspend the legislative procedure and the issue will be referred to the BCR government for arbitration. Then, the proposed law, possibly amended by the government, is again submitted to the parliament for a vote.[42] The alarm bell is similar in nature to the 'petitions of concern' in the Northern Ireland Assembly, which give each community group a veto over certain issues.

Several mechanisms protecting the Dutch-speaking minority also exist at the government level. Articles 34 and 35 of the 1989 Brussels Act set the rules for the election of the government in the BCR. The government comprises one minister-president and four ministers. The BCR government respects the parity inasmuch as it is constituted of two ministers belonging to the FSG and two ministers belonging to the DSG. In turn, the minister-president is considered to be neutral and above the separation into language groups.[43]

The government-making procedure in Brussels can be described as follows. In the days after elections, the party that has obtained the largest number of seats in parliament traditionally takes the initiative to organise consultations. It envisages possible coalitions and discusses with other parties a political program for the legislature. These discussions also address the question of the constitution of a government. Once an agreement is reached on a governing coalition, a list including the five candidates for minister[44] must be presented to parliament. In order to be adopted, this list has to be supported by the majority of the deputies in the whole parliament, as well as by a majority within each language group. Given that this list is the result of negotiations between political parties after the elections, the likely success of forming a government is uncertain. For this reason, article 35, paragraph 2 of the 1989 Brussels Act provides a default solution in case parties fail to reach such an agreement. Under this default solution, each of the four ministers is elected in a different voting round by the majority of the parliament after having been supported by a majority within the language group to which it belongs. In turn, the minister-president of the Brussels government is elected by a majority of the parliament after having collected five signatures from parliament members. Interestingly enough, the 2001 Lombard agreement has provided for a default solution to this default solution. The threat of institutional stalemates resulting from the growing representation of the Vlaams Blok forced the democratic parties to envisage remedies to a blockage of the government-making procedure by the far right party. Hence, if no majority is reached within the language groups, and the default solution does not enable the community groups to appoint their ministers, another vote is held at least 30 days later. This time, while the candidates for the FSG must still be supported by a majority of their members, the candidates for the Dutch-speaking side have to be supported by a majority of the members of the FCC and no longer of the DSG.[45] Note that neither the default solution nor its spare solution have been implemented yet.

With respect to the allocation of the portfolios within the government, the Dutch-speaking minority also benefits from certain protections. Indeed, if an agreement on this subject matter is not forthcoming, article 37 of the 1989 Brussels Act provides for a spare solution. This provision determines the competences of the five different ministries[46] and describes the allocation process. Under this subsidiary procedure, the minister-president is the first to choose which pre-determined competences it wants to exert; the two members of the FSG choose their preferred competences in second and fourth position and the two ministers from the DSG choose in third and fifth position (Lagasse 2003: 177). This procedure should guarantee that the Dutch-speaking ministers are not allocated so-called empty portfolios.

Finally, decision-making procedure within the government provides also for some protection to the Dutch-speaking minority. Collegiality and consensus are followed as a rule of thumb. This means that every minister has *de facto* informal veto power (Coffé 2006: 101). The objective of these measures is to integrate the community groups and political parties and to create a climate of cooperation rather than defiance and competition (Lijphart 2004: 101).

The current institutional structure in Brussels is thus characterised by numerous minority protection mechanisms at both the parliament level and the government level. These protection mechanisms often entail co-decision proceedings, and thus a kind of veto power for both community groups. In the BCR, they have resulted in a rather successful form of cooperation by both ethno-linguistic groups and indeed in a smooth co-administration of the region. In other words, the minority protection mechanisms promote positive incentives for inter-ethnic cooperation and encourage political moderation. All in all, this system invites community groups to go beyond their differences.

Overall, this section has highlighted the BCR's remarkable capacity to adapt to political, economic and sociological evolutions and to do so with an equally remarkable low level of hostility between community groups. These achievements were certainly made possible thanks to mechanisms guaranteeing a combination of protection of the Dutch-speaking minority and a sufficient level of cooperation between community groups. Together these two characteristics, adaptability and cooperation, make the BCR a dynamic model of power-sharing. Consociationalism in the BCR seems indeed to be *living consociationalism*.

'Living consociationalism' in the BCR

Over their almost 30 years of existence, the BCR institutions have displayed a remarkable capacity to peacefully adapt to evolving political demands raised by the French-speaking and Dutch-speaking groups and, in doing so, to tone down the tensions between these community groups. The consociational arrangements in Brussels have indeed evolved at the rhythm of several institutional reforms. In that sense, consociationalism in Brussels is *living consociationalism*. Now, what are the features of the BCR that have been decisive in its ability to serenely evolve over time and to adapt to changing demands? What are the characteristics of living consociationalism in Brussels? And what are the challenges the BCR faces, and which could call for future adjustments of its institutions?

In the following section we reflect upon the observations made on the Brussels case, and we formulate the concept of *living consociationalism*. Then we discuss potential institutional challenges to the BCR.

BCR as an example of 'living consociationalism': adaptability and cooperation

It seems that the achievements of the BCR are of a double nature. First, it has been able to address the community groups' demands for institutional changes. Second, the institutional setting has largely managed to capture and absorb the tensions between community groups so that frictions did not turn violent but remained at the institutional level. Several mechanisms have facilitated this double performance; key among them are the articulate set of legal procedures for the reform of the institutions and the mechanisms providing for cooperation in BCR institutions.

To begin with, the capacity of the BCR power-sharing arrangements to adapt over time was influenced by the nature of the legal procedures for institutional revisions. These procedures indeed represent a subtle equilibrium between flexibility and rigidity.

Flexibility is guaranteed by the several variants that exist for the reform of the institutions: the revision of the Constitution, the adoption of special acts and the adoption of special ordonnances. As already explained, each legal instrument relates to matters of different nature and of different importance. Accordingly, the procedure for the adoption of each of these instruments is more or less demanding. The progressivity of these three types of procedures can be seen as three steps in a staircase. Together they ensure that the most fundamental institutional aspects of the Belgian federal structure have the most demanding revision procedures. Correlatively, the less fundamental the reform, the less constraining the revision procedure. In this way, Brussels' adoption of a staircase model guarantees certain flexibility. This incremental approach plays an important role in its capacity to adapt to the evolving demands of the community groups. These micro-institutional mechanisms (demonstrated in Figure 2.2) could provide additional safeguards for the viability of peace settlements, and, as we demonstrate in the chapter on Cyprus, could be particularly relevant in supporting power-sharing mediations.

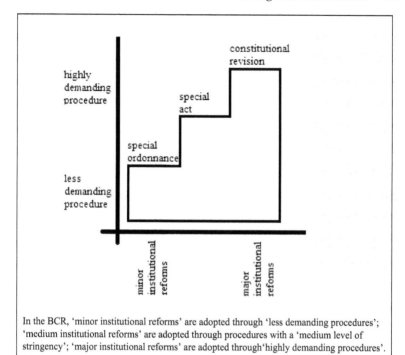

In the BCR, 'minor institutional reforms' are adopted through 'less demanding procedures'; 'medium institutional reforms' are adopted through procedures with a 'medium level of stringency'; 'major institutional reforms' are adopted through 'highly demanding procedures'.

Figure 2.2 The staircase model: equilibrium between flexibility and rigidity for institutional reforms in the BCR

The staircase model of the BCR allows for a clear distinction between various levels of demands, and in each case determines an appropriate procedure. In this context, a demand of minor importance would not be subjected to an overly constraining procedure. Conversely, a fundamental institutional change cannot be adopted through the least demanding procedure. This second assertion shows how the staircase model for institutional reforms in Brussels in fact accounts for flexibility but also, to a certain extent, for rigidity, by funnelling more fundamental changes through more demanding procedures. In Brussels, the adoption of a staircase model thus guarantees a subtle balance between flexibility and rigidity for institutional reforms. The first stage of the federalisation process, the 1970 reform of the institutions, which included article 107 quarter on the existence of three regions in the Constitution, was realised through constitutional reform. Then the *de facto* creation of the BCR and the 2001 and 2011–2012 reforms were undertaken through the adoption of special acts. More recently, special ordonnances have been used as instruments for organizational changes in the BCR.

Next to the articulate set of legal procedures guaranteeing adaptability in BCR, another type of mechanism has facilitated the success of the BCR evolution: cooperation mechanisms.

The capture and absorption of inter-community tensions is undertaken in Brussels through the provision of strong protection mechanisms for the Dutch-speaking minority, as well as through a high degree of cooperation required from both community groups. As already mentioned above, both aspects are in fact the two sides of the same coin. The protection mechanisms for the Dutch-speaking minority – such as guaranteed representation in the parliament and the government, parity within the government, the double majority ordonnance, the alarm bell procedure, and so on – require the French-speaking majority to adopt a cooperative approach. Indeed, in order to be endorsed, a political reform will most likely require the support of both language groups. Furthermore, in the BCR, cooperation between community groups materialises in mechanisms such as the collegiality and the consensus rules for the adoption of decisions at the government level. The kind of veto power each minister has constitutes a strong incentive for cooperation.

Together, the flexibility and rigidity provided by the rules for reform of the BCR institutions and the cooperation mechanisms contribute to the Brussels institutions' capacity to peacefully adapt to evolving political demands raised by the French-speaking and Dutch-speaking groups, and to tone down the tensions between these community groups. The analysis of the BCR model demonstrates how institutional arrangements have been lively and indeed, how they account for living consociationalism.

Consociational arrangements are traditionally seen as power-sharing arrangements with direct representation and participation of the main community groups in the administration of public institutions. Consociational arrangements set the rules that define the decision-making process and allocate decision-making rights to different community groups in divided societies (Hartzell, Hoddie 2003: 320; McCulloch,& McGarry 2017: 1–4). The addition of the epithet 'living' before the notion of consociationalism accounts for the idea that consociational arrangements are situational. They address a specific sociological and political situation. This situation is, however, likely to evolve over time. The different groups constituting the divided society change in relative size. The nature of their political demands shifts. Their degree of satisfaction with respect to the institutional framework in which they operate fluctuates, and so on. In short, the preferences of community groups in divided societies are subject to a complex and continuously evolving set of political, economic and sociological variables. For these reasons, it seems that consociational arrangements in deeply divided societies are likely to be exposed to demands for adjustment. *Living consociationalism* accounts for the latter and postulates that these arrangements need to include procedural and cooperation mechanisms that enable institutions to adapt over time.

At the core of *living consociationalism* is the simple idea that divided societies are in constant transformation and that these transformations call for institutional adaptations. From that simple concept results two essential characteristics of *living consociationalism*: first, the capacity for institutional arrangements in divided societies to adapt to changing community groups' demands related to non-fixed political, economic and sociological situations in order to prevent possible confrontations between community groups; and second, to do so in a peaceful way. In the BCR this has been possible thanks to the flexibility and rigidity of the staircase model for institutional reforms and through cooperation mechanisms. Living consociationalism acknowledges the fragility and the essentially conjunctural nature of consociational arrangements and provides the institutional tools, both legally and politically, that are necessary to address institutional challenges. It is thus not so much the absence of crises but the capacity to address them peacefully that characterizes living consociationalism.

By providing a combination of flexible procedures for institutional reforms with an extensive set of institutional incentives for cooperation between community groups, the BCR model is thus a prototypical example of living consociationalism. Now, potential institutional challenges to the BCR institutions still exist. In the next paragraphs, we discuss two of these challenges which could possibly require the BCR to, once again, prove its capacity to adapt to evolving situations.

Institutional challenges in the BCR

The BCR repeatedly managed to address the structural issues it faced. However, challenges with the potential to act as destabilizing factors in the relations between Brussels' two community groups still exist. Two of these factors are discussed in the following paragraphs: the disproportional representation of the ethno-linguistic groups in the BCR parliament and the relation of these groups with their community groups in the Belgian context. These two aspects represent challenges that could call for future adjustments of the BCR institutions.

Considering the importance in divided societies of group representation, the BCR offers an interesting case study. It has indeed implemented two alternative models of representation since its creation in 1989. The first model, applied from 1989 until 2004, opted for a 'proportional representation' of the community groups in parliament. Since 2004, proportional representation has been swapped for a system of 'disproportional representation'. Accordingly, the number of seats the FSG and the DSG receive within the BCR parliament is no longer strictly proportional to the share of votes each community group obtains at the regional elections. As such, the new system raises questions of compliance with basic legal principles. The current form of guaranteed representation could therefore be the object of future institutional reforms.

Originally, the BCR parliament had 75 seats and was divided into two language groups. The number of seats each of these groups received depended on the proportion of votes each of them obtained in regional elections. The number of seats allocated to the language groups was thus meant to vary across elections and to enable a strict proportional representation of each community group.[47] The issue of weak DSG representation in the BCR parliament was raised during the negotiations of the 2001 Lombard agreement, and a revision of the representation model in Brussels was called for. A solution was eventually enacted in the 2001 Lombard agreement, which at the request of the Volksunie swapped proportional representation for guaranteed DSG representation.

More specifically, the system of parliamentary seat allocation was revised in two ways. The first modification concerned the increase in the number of seats from 75 to 89. The second consisted of the replacement of strict proportional representation by a system of guaranteed representation. From then on, regardless of the number of people having voted for lists belonging to the FSG or the DSG, the two groups receive a fixed number of seats – 72 seats for the FSG and 17 for the DSG. In turn, the allocation of seats *within* each language group is determined by the electoral results according to the proportionality rule. In other words, proportional representation is no longer assured *between* language groups, but only between political parties *within* each language group. All in all, these adjustments enable a larger and more refined representation of the political sensibilities in the DSG in Brussels and a spread of the workload over a larger number of deputies.

Another important effect of adopting a system of guaranteed representation is that it reinforces the position of the DSG in Brussels. The allocation key of 72/17 used since the 2004 elections is indeed clearly strengthening the representation of the DSG with respect to the real share of votes they receive at the elections. The new article 20 of the 1989 Brussels Act provides that an electoral divider – that is, the quotient between the number of votes cast by a language group and the number of seats allocated to this group – determines the number of seats each list receives. In this framework, it is noteworthy that the number of voices required for a list to be allocated a seat – in other words, the electoral divider – is much higher in the FSG than the DSG. In fact, while 5,433 voters in 2004; 5,679 voters in 2009; and 5,681 voters in 2014 were necessary for a list of the FSG to obtain a seat, the number was substantially lower for lists belonging to the

Table 2.1 Data on the BCR elections

	Regional elections of 1989		Regional elections of 1995		Regional elections of 1999		Regional elections of 2004		Regional elections of 2009		Regional elections of 2014	
Seats allocated to the FSG and percentage	64	85%	65	87%	64	85%	72	81%	72	81%	72	81%
Seats allocated to the DSG and percentage	11	15%	10	13%	11	15%	17	19%	17	19%	17	19%
Votes cast for the FSG and percentage	371.192	85%	356.231	86%	366.195	86%	391.216	86%	408.870	89%	409.048	88%
Votes cast for the DSG and percentage	67.000	15%	56.746	14%	60.546	14%	62.516	14%	51.818	11%	53.379	12%
Electoral divider for the FSG							391.216/72=5.433		408.870/72=5.679		409.048/72=5.681	
Electoral divider for the DSG							62.516/17=3.677		51.818/17=3.084		53.379/17=3.139	

Source: Data retrieved from http://ibsa.brussels/themes/elections/elections-1#.WbeHpfNJbIU.

DSG, namely 3,677 in 2004; 3,084 in 2009; and 3,139 in 2014. These observations imply that, in Brussels, citizens' voting power varies depending on whether they vote for lists belonging to the FSG or to the DSG. In turn, this unequal voting power raises essential questions of fairness and of compliance with basic legal principles.

A case was launched before the Belgian Constitutional Court to challenge the principle of guaranteed representation in Brussels. The allocation of a fixed number of seats to each language group, part of the special act of 13 June 2001 modifying article 20 of the 1989 Brussels Act, was indeed disputed before the Belgian jurisdiction on the ground that it potentially violates the principles of equality and of non-discrimination, as well as the principle of free and equal voting guaranteed under articles 10 and 11 of the Belgian Constitution, article 14 of the European Convention on Human Rights and article 25 of the 1966 International Covenant on Civil and Political Rights (Dumont 2002: 30–31; Uyttendaele 2002: 204).

In the 35/2003 decision of 25 March 2003, the Court acknowledged that the principle of proportional representation is indeed potentially distorted in Brussels. It considers, however, that this distortion does not constitute a violation of the fundamental principles of equality and non-discrimination. It justifies its decision by arguing that the protections given to the Dutch-speaking minority in Brussels should be understood in the larger Belgian federal context, implying that the French-speaking minority benefits from similar protections at the federal level.[48]

This decision was adopted in 2003. The regional elections that have taken place since have displayed a substantial distortion of the system in favour of the DSG. This distortion is the result of mechanisms intended to protect the Dutch-speaking minority in the BCR. Therefore, the system implemented in the BCR has also been called the 'protective dis-proportional representation model' (Bodson, Loizides 2017). Future sociological evolutions in the form of an increasing imbalance between these community groups in Brussels could put the system of guaranteed representation under even stronger pressure.[49] These socio-legal tensions probably represent one of the most significant current challenges to the consociational arrangements in Brussels.

Another serious challenge is that of the interaction between community groups within the broader national context. Inter-group relations in Brussels are indeed affected by the way each community group relates to the member of its ethno-linguistic group outside Brussels as well as by the overall relation between community groups in Belgium.

The political crisis that stalled the French-speaking part of Belgium during the summer of 2017 is a good example of how group relations in Brussels can be affected by external aspects. It shows indeed that the relations between political parties within a language group can affect the subtle equilibrium reached within the BCR institutions.

Repeated scandals of corruption and fundamental breaches of good governance principles within the French-speaking socialist party, PS, have affected the readiness of its governing partner, the French-speaking Christian Democrat Party, cdH, to continue to govern together for the rest of the 2014–2019 legislature.[50] The lack of trust between these two French-speaking parties has not only affected the government of the Walloon region and that of the French-speaking community, but has also contaminated the Brussels government, where they sit together in the governing coalition. The difficulty for the cdH to shape an alternative coalition in the BCR has however, forced both parties to continue governing together in the Brussels region.[51] In order to find an alternative governing coalition, parties must indeed gather at least 37 of the 72 seats allocated to the FSG. Now, the distribution of seats within the BCR parliament and the political lines of the different parties made it very difficult for the cdH to find such alternative majority.

This crisis highlights both the way in which politics in the BCR can be influenced by the political life outside the region, as well as the absence of mechanisms to address and diffuse political tensions between collation partners in Brussels. The difficulty in finding a solution to such institutional stalemate could, as in the case for guaranteed representation in Brussels, lead to further adjustments of the BCR institutions.

Conclusion

In the first chapter, it was argued that further adjustments of institutions in Northern Ireland are inevitable, and that these reforms can put the fragile equilibrium between communities at risk. The Brussels Capital Region offers a second case of interest for the general issue addressed by this book on the capacity of institutional arrangements in divided societies to adapt to changing political circumstances.

The BCR offers an example of *living consociationalism*. The concept of *living consociationalism* captures the regions' remarkable capacity both to adapt to evolving demands raised by its two ethno-linguistic groups and to keep the inter-community tensions at a very low level. The BCR indeed displays an elegant combination of flexible procedures for institutional reforms with an extensive set of institutional incentives for cooperation between community groups. We argued in this chapter that this double achievement makes the BCR a more dynamic form of power-sharing compared to the model adopted in Northern Ireland.

In order to introduce this analysis, we began with a description of the broader institutional framework in which the BCR institutions should be understood, namely the Belgian federal structure. Since 1970, the Belgian institutions have evolved from a unitary state to a three-tiered federal state with communities, regions and a federal level. This evolution has largely been the result of persistent tensions between the two main ethno-linguistic groups of Belgium and their demand for some degree of autonomy.

Having established the principal characteristics of the Belgian federal structure, the next section focused on the BCR system. The creation and evolution of the BCR institutions were discussed in more detail. This discussion singled out the BCR's capacity to transform and adapt to new political and sociological situations. The current design of the Brussels institutions was then presented. This presentation highlighted the importance of the mechanisms protecting the Dutch-speaking minority, and the related necessity for community groups to cooperate in Brussels. It was argued in this section that the BCR has generally displayed a rare ability to address the demands of the different community groups and to peacefully adapt over time.

The discussion of the BCR institutions was then used in the last section to illustrate the central characteristics of *living consociationalism*. It was argued that the concept of *living consociationalism* is rooted in the idea that institutional arrangements in deeply divided societies are situational. They address sociological and political relations in a specific moment. This situation is, however, likely to evolve over time. In the BCR, this evolution was linked both to the general process of federalisation and to variables unique to Brussels. The economic variables were, *inter alia*, the demands to refinance the FsCC and to better equip Brussels to manage its economic leadership by the creation of the 'Brussels community'. The political variables related to the weak representation of the DSG and the problems it entailed for its deputies, as well as issues raised by the growing importance of the Vlaams Blok within the BCR parliament, the demand for constitutive autonomy, and so on. Finally, the sociological variable was represented by the need to address the population's demand for constitutive autonomy, by the adoption of guaranteed representation, and by many protection mechanisms guaranteed to the DSG. Together these political, economic and sociological variables are the salt of the Brussels Capital Region's life.

In common with the previous chapter on Northern Ireland, this analysis provides an example of the capacity of consociational systems to move beyond their accommodationist foundations into a more integrated space – designated in the previous chapter as accommodation+. In the BCR context, both ethno-linguistic groups were able to build a common purpose and define themselves and their inter-group partners as being involved in the same political project with similar goals – despite remaining distinctly between language communities. In the next chapter, we will see how Cyprus has struggled with the implementation and renegotiation of a power-sharing agreement and how some of the micro-institutional details emerging from the Northern Ireland and Brussels cases could inspire optimism for future mediations. As such, Cyprus offers yet another example of how institutions in divided societies could face prohibitive conditions, particularly in the early mediation stages.

Notes

1 Dutch was eventually adopted as the second official language in 1898.
2 Note that the German-speaking area of Belgium was re-annexed to Germany by Hitler's regime from 1940 until 1945. After the 1945 armistice it returned to Belgium.
3 The Belgian population amounts to a total of 11,304,000. The Dutch-speaking region comprises 57.59% of the overall population; the French-speaking region 31.26%; the German-speaking region 0.68%; and the bilingual region of Brussels-Capital (French and Dutch) 10.47 %. Statistics were established on 1 January 2017 and retrieved from the website of the Belgian 'Service Public Fédéral Intérieur': www.ibz.rrn.fgov.be/fileadmin/user_upload/fr/pop/statistiques/population-bevolking-20170101.pdf
4 There exists, however, some municipalities along the 'language border' between Flanders and Wallonia, between the French-speaking region and the German-speaking region, and around Brussels where, because of the substantial presence of members of the other community group, the population benefits from so-called language facilities. On demand, they can receive the administrative documents in their own language.
5 Of the Flemish population, 52.5% considers itself to have a good or very good knowledge of French; 15.5% of the population in Wallonia say that they have a good or very good knowledge of Dutch; and 29% of the population in Brussels considers itself as having a good or very good knowledge of 'the other language'.
6 This philosophical divide led to punctual clashes such as the 1958 'School Pact issue' on the subvention of confessional and non-confessional schools by public authorities. In the School Pact issue, the traditional opposition between community groups was complicated by one about philosophical obedience.
7 Statistics retrieved from the website of the Belgian Agency for Statistics http://statbel.fgov.be/fr/statistiques/chiffres/travailvie/emploi/relatifs/
8 The figures on external trade should be read in parallel to those with the repartition of the population on the Belgian territory (see above). Statistics retrieved from www.flandersinvestmentandtrade.com/en/news/flemish-exports-reach-new-historic-high, and from http://ec.europa.eu/eurostat/data/database
9 Demands for separatism have a long history in Belgium and were raised within both community groups. Note that article 1 of the status of the NV-A, a Flemish nationalist party and currently the largest political force in Flanders, provides that the party strives towards the independence of Flanders.
10 The language act of 1962 provided for the transfer of several municipalities located in Flanders to Wallonia and vice versa. This transfer fostered many reactions from the most radical groups. Amongst them, the Taal Actie Komitee, a

nationalist group opposing the presence of French-speakers in Flanders, organised regular demonstrations, some of which were occasionally violent.

11   The Catholic University of Leuven is located in Flanders. In 1968 its board of directors decided, under pressure of the population, to adopt Dutch as the main teaching language. French-speaking students who had been taking courses mainly taught in French were then urged to leave the city under the slogan 'Walen Buiten' (literally, 'Walloon get out of here'). A new university was built shortly after in Louvain-la-Neuve, in Wallonia, where courses are taught in French.

12   Note that the Flemish region was directly absorbed by the Flemish community. Both entities thus have the same parliament and the same government. They do, however, keep a separate legal personality. See article 3 of the of the Special Act of 8 August 1980 on the Institutional Reforms. This evolution along the Flemish side makes for an asymmetrical federal structure in Belgium.

13   For a more detailed discussion of the six state's reforms, see Uyttendaele 2014.

14   For a detailed enumeration of the regions' competences, see article 6 and followings of the Special Act of 8 August 1980 on the Institutional Reforms.

15   For a detailed enumeration of the communities' competences, see articles 4, 5, 6 bis and followings of the Special Act of 8 August 1980 on the Institutional Reforms.

16   See article 35 of the Constitution.

17   In practice, such conflicts are, however, frequent. In order to prevent them, the Concertation Committee, the State Council and the Constitutional Court can intervene *ex ante* or *ex post* to solve or decide on possible conflicts of competences between the different entities in Belgium.

18   A discussion of the transfer of competences is left aside.

19   This approximate ratio is based on an analysis of the votes cast at the BCR regional elections since 1989.

20   Over the past century, the city shifted from being one where Dutch was the language spoken by a majority of the population to one in which only a very limited minority would use this language on a daily basis. The worry of a proliferation of this dynamic of 'Frenchisation' into further areas within Flanders strongly motivated the Dutch-speaking community group's demand to tie the Brussels institutions to those of the communities.

21   In fact, Wilfried Maertens was prime minster of Belgium since 1979. He had only been replaced during a period of eight months in 1981 by the Flemish Christian Democrat Gaston Eyskens.

22   The community groups also agreed on the enlargement of the control scope of the Arbitration Court.

23   Article 23 of the 1989 Brussels Act.

24   Article 6 of the Special Act of 8 August 1980 on the Institutional Reforms.

25   These entities are established by article 60 of the 1989 Brussels Act. The FsCC, the FCC and the CCC have each their own assembly and executive. While the FCC assembly comprises the 17 members of the DSG plus 5 additional members, the FsCC assembly consists of the 72 members of the FSG and the CCC of the 89 members of the BCR parliament. The FsCC and the FCC are subordinated and complete the French-speaking and the Flemish communities. Overall, the communities and community commissions are in charge of culture, education and health and well-being policies for organisations affiliated to their respective language group in Brussels.

26 See, *inter alia*, the governmental declaration of 7 July 1999.
27 Specialised commissions are often created by the federal government in order to conduct negotiations on institutional reforms in Belgium. This strategy is utilised to diffuse political pressures and to keep the federal government out of jeopardy. On this technique of 'encommissioning', see Bourgaux 2003. Note that the Vlaams Blok was thus not invited to take part to the negotiations.
28 The assembly counts 15 different commissions. The participation of the members of the DSG in these commissions could therefore only amount to a maximum of two deputies, with one of them often being a member of the Vlaams Blok.
29 At the 1989 regional elections, the Vlaams Blok received 1 of the 10 seats allocated to the DSG; then 2 of 11 in 1995 and 4 of 10 in 1999. The political weight of the Vlaams Blok thus steadily increased over the 1990s. Given the firm refusal of democratic parties to associate with the Vlaams Blok, one more seat for the far-right party in 1999 could have led to a paralysis of the BCR institutions. The institutional threat represented by the Vlaams Blok was bent down at the following regional elections. It obtained 6 seats of 17 in 2004, 3 seats in 2009 and 1 seat in 2014.
30 The 2001 Lambermont agreement was adopted on the French-speaking side by the PRL, PS and Ecolo, and on the Dutch-speaking side by the VLD-VU-O and SP.AGA. It was rejected by the French-speaking parties PSC and FDF and by the Dutch-speaking party CVP.
31 Article 92 bis, paragraph 7 of the Special Act of 8 August 1980 on the Institutional Reforms.
32 The BCR is now in charge, *inter alia*, of tourism (article 6, paragraph 1, VI, first line of the Special Act of 8 August 1980 on the Institutional Reforms), bi-cultural matters of regional interest, and so forth. For more information, see Lievens 2014.
33 Article 118 of the Constitution provides for the principle of constitutive autonomy.
34 Under article 138 of the Constitution, the French-speaking community can decide to transfer some of its competences to the Walloon region as well as to the FsCC. The BCR constitutive autonomy regarding competences is thus limited in the sense that it concerns competences of the French-speaking community that can only be transferred, provided the agreement between the three entities: the French-speaking community, the Walloon region and the FsCC.
35 For a detailed enumeration of the matters encompassed in the BCR constitutive autonomy, see article 28 of the 1989 Brussels Act.
36 See article 28 of the 1989 Brussels Act.
37 Article 3 of the Constitution.
38 Special ordonnance of 4 June 2015. This special ordonnance fixed the beginning of the 2015–2016 parliamentary year in Brussels.
39 As confirmed in the parliamentary documents, Ann. Parl., Sénat, 18 juin 1970, p. 2011.
40 Article 35 of the Special Act of 8 August 1980 on the Institutional Reforms states that, unless otherwise provided, the BCR parliament can take decisions if a majority of its members are present. In turn, to be adopted, a decision needs to gather the majority of the expressed votes. Article 28 of the Brussels Act further constraints this absolute majority procedure. For a limited list of matters, article 28 states indeed that a majority also needs to be obtained within each language

group. In certain cases it couples this condition to that of a two-thirds majority overall, and so on.

41 Article 31 of the 1989 Brussels Act.

42 The good cooperation between both linguistic groups in Brussels makes it quite unlikely for the alarm bell procedure to be activated in the near future. This procedure also exists at the federal level, where it was already actioned twice.

43 Coffé and Uyttendaele have diverging opinions in that regard. For a discussion of the notion of parity with the BCR government, see Uyttendaele 2014, pp. 189–190; Coffé 2006, p. 101.

44 It is noteworthy that next to the minister-president and his or her four ministers, the BCR executive also includes three state secretaries. The state secretaries are in charge of secondary competences and are attached to one minister. At least one of the state secretaries has to come from the DSG.

45 The assembly of the FCC includes the 17 members of the DSG plus five additional members from the Flemish parliament. See article 60 bis of the 1989 Brussels Act. This measure was taken in order to avoid potential political stalemates created in Brussels by the strong representation of the Vlaams Blok.

46 For a description of these competences, see article 37 of the 1989 Brussels Act.

47 The fact that, in order to be considered for the seats allocation, a list needs to gather at lesat 5% of the votes within its language group, is left aside.

48 Note that under article 63 of the Constitution, the linguistic groups in the federal parliament receive a number of seats proportional to their share. Therefore, the French-speaking minority at the federal level does not benefit from a system of guaranteed representation, as is the case for the Dutch-speaking minority in Brussels. Moreover, this decision was taken before the first application of the new electoral model at the 2004 regional elections. It is thus questionable whether the Constitutional Court had the capacity to assess the scope of the distortion of the electoral divider on both sides.

49 Note that voting is mandatory in Belgium, so the data displayed in Table 2.1 gives a relatively reliable representation of the evolution of the size of the language groups in Brussels.

50 These scandals related to the bad governance of the nonprofit organisation Samusocial, an organization bringing relief to homeless people in the city of Brussels; Nethys, a Belgian group active in the energy sector, and so on.

51 They constitute the governing coalition for the 2014–2019 legislature in the BCR together with DeFi in the FSG and with Open-VLD, CD&V and SP.A on the Dutch-speaking side.

Bibliography

Bodson, T. & Loizides, N. (2017) 'Consociationalism in the Brussels Capital Region: Dis-Proportional Representation and the Accommodation of National Minorities'. In McCulloch, A. & McGarry, J. (Eds.): *Power Sharing. Empirical and Normative Challenges*: Taylor & Francis.

Bourgaux, A-E (2003) L'évolution des modes de négociation institutionnelle ou la machine à explorer le temps institutionnel belge. In *Les Accords du Lambermont et du Lombard, Editions. ULB Centre de droit public*, pp. 22–60.

Bruycker, P. de (1989) Bruxelles dans la réforme de l'Etat. In *Courrier hebdomadaire du CRISP* (5), pp. 1–61.

Coffé, H. (2006) 'The vulnerable institutional complexity'the 2004 regional elections in Brussels. In *Regional & Federal Studies* 16 (1), pp. 99–107.

Delwit, P & Hellings, B. (2001): Les accords du Lambermont – Saint-Polycarpe. In *L'année sociale* 2002, pp. 43–54.

Dumont, H. (2002) Les Problèmes Méthodologiques. In Francis Delpérée (Ed.): Les lois spéciales et ordinaire du 13 juillet 2001. La réforme de la Saint-Polycarpe: Bruylant.

Hartzell, C., & Hoddie, M. (2003) 'Institutionalizing Peace. Power Sharing and Post-Civil War Conflict Management.' *American Journal of Political Science* 47 (2): 318–332.

Hepburn, A. C. (2004) *Contested cities in the modern West*: Springer.

Lagasse, N. (2003) Les Accords dits du Lombard. In Université libre de Bruxelles, Centre de droit public: Les accords du Lambermont et du Lombard. Approfondissement du fédéralisme ou erreur d'aiguillage?: colloque organisé le 22 février 2002: Bruylant.

Lievens, J. (2014) Brussel volgens de Zesde Staatshervorming: formidable of fort minable? In Instituut voor Constitutioneel Recht Colloquium (Ed.): Het federale België na de Zesde Staatshervorming: die Keure.

Lijphart, A. (2004) 'Constitutional Design for Divided Societies.' *Journal of Democracy* 15 (2): 96–109.

McCulloch, A., & McGarry, J. (Eds.) (2017) *Power Sharing. Empirical and Normative Challenges*: Taylor & Francis.

Nassaux, J-P. (2000) Le groupe de travail sur le fonctionnement des institutions bruxelloises. Première phase: oct. 1999-mai 2000: Centre de recherche et d'information socio-politiques (CRISP).

Nassaux, J-P. (2001) Le groupe de travail sur le fonctionnement des institutions bruxelloises. Deuxième phase et accord dit du Lombard: Centre de recherche et d'information socio-politiques.

Uyttendaele, M. (2002) Les Accords du Lombard. Entre le Reflexe Salutaire et le Salmigondis Institutionnel. In Francis Delpérée (Ed.): Les lois spéciales et ordinaire du 13 juillet 2001. La réforme de la Saint-Polycarpe: Bruylant.

Uyttendaele, M. (2014) Les institutions de la Belgique: Primento.

van Parys, J. & Wauters, S. (2006): Les connaissances linguistiques en Belgique. In *Cahier du CEREC* 31.

3 A federal Cyprus?
Integrating alternative power-sharing models

Introduction

This chapter aims to integrate previous power-sharing models in the discussion of consociational designs proposed in the Cyprus peace talks over the past decades. Focusing on UN proposals, the chapter addresses their most problematic features and suggests an alternative power-sharing system based on the achievements of other divided societies, specifically the Northern Ireland (NI) case and the Brussels Capital Region (BCR) model discussed extensively in the two preceding chapters. As mentioned, the d'Hondt system is a power-sharing innovation that has contributed to broad inclusive coalitions and political stability in Northern Ireland since 2007 (O'Leary et al 2005; McGarry and O'Leary, 2009). The Brussels Capital Region model, meanwhile, provides a set of intriguing institutional innovations, including a two-tier system where failure to form a voluntary coalition between majorities in the two main French-speakingand Dutch-speaking community groups could lead to a grand coalition appointed independently by each side. By creating incentives for wider participation across political parties in government, the NI and BCR models avoid a problematic and time-consuming aspect of consociationalism – forming inter-ethnic majority coalitions. As the chapter explains, such broadly inclusive parliamentary systems could be relevant for Cyprus, fitting nicely with the specific features and needs of Cypriot political parties and replacing current (not-agreed-upon) proposals.

This chapter expands arguments made in the introduction on the role of 'mediation' and 'informality' in consociations and applies both themes to Cyprus. Mediation focuses on the need for negotiability, an aspect frequently under-emphasised in the literature (for exceptions, see McGarry & Loizides, 2015; Loizides, 2014; McGarry 2017). Informality departs from conventional wisdom in the study of the island's protracted mediations and failures: while most scholars and practitioners consider Cyprus a failed case of international mediation, we argue that since the island's accession to the EU, the two communities have developed a number of early proto-consociational structures. Although they do not offer a substitute for the formal consociational arrangements, these early political initiatives, movements and structures tell a theoretically insightful story on informal power-sharing of relevance to other *de facto* partitioned places. This growth of informal, or 'creeping', consociationalism has been seen in the other two cases in the book and relates back to the title of this text: *Mediating Power-Sharing*. The structures of consociationalism have evolved informally as well as formally over time. In the NI context the basis for power-sharing was set out in the Belfast/Good Friday Agreement (GFA) as highlighted in Chapter 1, but over time this was supplemented as a consequence of further political negotiations and agreements, notably the St Andrews Agreement (2006), the Stormont House Agreement (2014) and the Fresh Start agreement (2015). The BCR form of consociationalism has also been mediated through several iterations over time as outlined in the previous chapter. The Cyprus case examined in this chapter demonstrates the ways in which informal models of consociationalism could help transform a prolonged, frozen and intransigent conflict into a prospective candidate for a larger scale formal power-sharing.

Cyprus from power-sharing to partition

Cyprus escaped the devastating wars of the late Ottoman era, as it was transferred to the British by the 1878 Berlin Congress. Turkey recognized the 1914 annexation of the island by the British in the 1923 Treaty of Lausanne (article 20), and it became a Crown colony in 1925. The first decades of colonial rule saw minimal conflict, but both Greek and Turkish Cypriots gradually developed stronger attachments to their respective 'motherlands' and became more assertive in their ethnopolitical demands (Demetriou 2012). Greek Cypriots have historically taken a majoritarian and pro-Hellenic perspective in their aspirations, pointing not only to their demographic stature (historically about 80% of the population) but also to the significant Greek and Greek Cypriot contributions in the Second World War. Turkish Cypriot counter-mobilisations emphasised previous ownership of the island, geographic proximity to Turkey and, more importantly, inter-communal fear. Turkish Cypriots saw, and continue to see, the Greek Cypriot desire for *enosis* (union of Cyprus and Greece) as an existential threat given the history of the region.[1] In response to the post-war *enosis* movement, Turkish Cypriots, with the backing of Turkey, sought *taksim* (partition) of Cyprus into two separate territories (Bahcheli 1972:60; Attalides 1977:78–86).

Between 1955 and 1959, the National Organization of Cypriot Fighters (EOKA) attempted to end colonial rule and to unite the island with Greece.

The EOKA leadership initially promised not to target the Turkish Cypriot community and avoided bicommunal incidents. Despite EOKA promises, however, in the eyes of Turkish Cypriots, maintaining colonial rule was preferable to living under a potentially hostile Greek administration. Following the start of the EOKA campaign, Turkish Cypriots actively sided with colonial authorities, filling in for Greek Cypriot police officers who had resigned from their positions (Ker-Lindsay 2004:16). According to Turkish Cypriot accounts, many expected that 'sooner or later the campaign of terror would be directed against the Turkish Cypriot community' (Necatigil 1989: 7). Indeed, three years later, in 1958, the conflict took a bicommunal turn, as EOKA retaliated against Turkish Cypriots supporting British authorities, triggering further attacks and counterattacks (Bahcheli 1972:55). Ankara and Turkish Cypriots aimed at preventing the island from being dominated by Greeks, insisting on no change to the status quo without their consent (Ertekün 1981:1–5; Necatigil 1989: 7–8). For Greek Cypriots, any abandonment of the *enosis* struggle was deemed as a betrayal of national aspirations and unfair given the undisputed demographic, historical and cultural arguments for union with Greece (Papadakis 1999: 25; Demetriou 2012).

The two competing views eventually led to neither *enosis* nor *taksim* but to a forced partnership in the form of an early consociational settlement stipulated in the 1959–1960 Zürich-London Agreements. This forced partnership in the newly independent Republic of Cyprus was imposed on the two communities by their respective 'motherlands' in the climate of the Cold War (Xydis 1973). As in the externally mediated Sunningdale Agreement for Northern Ireland (see Chapter 1 on the role of London and Dublin at the time), consociationalism in the Zürich-London accords proved to be short-lived. The agreements constituted the first and only power-sharing attempt in Cyprus, which lasted for just three years. Critics point to consociationalism itself as a cause of the failure, particularly the separate election of community leaders (i.e. a Greek Cypriot president and Turkish Cypriot vice-president voted on only in their respective communities), the mutual vetoes of the two leaders and the over-representation of the minority Turkish Cypriots in the cabinet and the civil service (Adams 1966; Polyviou 1980; Anderson 2008). As we demonstrated in the previous chapters, however, such features are prevalent in both the current political systems of Northern Ireland and the Brussels Capital Region, yet the results have been very different. Consociationalism could not have been solely at fault but some of its specific features might have contributed to the collapse. For instance, unlike BCR and Northern Ireland, Cyprus in the 1960s was a 'presidential consociation', a power-sharing system clearly disfavoured by consociational theorists advocating parliamentarianism (Lijphart, 1968, 1994, 2004; Linz 1990; McGarry 2011).

More importantly, as Lijphart (1977:160) argues, the main reason for the failure of consociationalism in Cyprus was that it could not be imposed against the wishes of one or more segments of a plural society, in particular against the majority community. In this respect, the Cypriot case parallels the Northern Ireland one discussed earlier in this book, with a dual imbalance of power constituting the crucially unfavourable factor (ibid; see also Trimikliniotis 2009). But as the example of Northern Ireland suggests, structural disadvantages do not always predetermine consociational failures, if institutions are designed to address or at least to mitigate such weaknesses.

A further factor worth mentioning across our cases is that timing of power-sharing agreements clearly plays some part in each society's capacity to develop a consensus agreement among parties and electorates. In the Cyprus case the timing has not always augmented the political space available for the parties to promote the consociational model effectively to their supporters. In the NI context, the original attempt to build a power-sharing Executive in 1974, following the Sunningdale Agreement of the previous year, failed after a few weeks, but not because of the internal dynamics of the consociational system or those involved in operating it. Its demise owed more to a lack of support within the unionist electorate, the mobilisation of spoiler groups on the unionist side – notably the grass-roots coalition of trade unionists, business leaders, politicians and loyalist paramilitaries who formed the Ulster Worker's Council (UWC). The decision by the UK government to hold a general election during this period also destabilised this embryonic attempt at power-sharing, as it forced the electorate to make a snap judgement before the benefits of power-sharing had really been felt. It also led to instability, as the Conservative government in London that had mediated the Sunningdale Agreement was defeated and replaced by a Labour administration with little political capital invested in the enterprise. This legacy in the NI context in part explains why a generation later in 1998, former SDLP leader Seamus Mallon referred to the power-sharing agreement that had been reached in the Multi-Party talks as 'Sunningdale for slow learners'. In short, the timing in 1998 was much more conducive to a consensus agreement than it was in 1974, despite the similarity of the power-sharing institutions that were agreed upon.

As with the NI example, a number of overarching geopolitical factors also worked against consociational success in Cyprus (and these continue to be a major cause for the failures to reunify Cyprus). For example, the Zürich-London Agreements institutionalised the military presence of Greece and Turkey in Cyprus as guarantor powers without their having to cooperate with the institutionalised structures of either NATO (as the original plan suggested) or with the limited UN forces post-1964 (Joseph 1997: 21; Necatigil 1989: 9–20; Loizides 2014).

Finally, in addition to the institutional and security reasons noted above, the collapse of the agreement was over-determined domestically by the fact that Greek Cypriots saw it as the first step towards *enosis*, while Turkish Cypriots continued to hold *taksim* as their priority. In the absence of effective and credible external guarantees, both communities remained captive to their fears of being pre-empted by the other (or by the 'motherlands'). As a result, both engaged in pre-emptive militarisation and violence, often with the explicit encouragement and sponsorship of Ankara and Athens, leading to the breakdown of consociational arrangements in 1963 and 1964. Thus, while Chapter 1 and Chapter 2 point to the often positive role external kin-state guarantees and involvement could have on local power-sharing, the Cypriot case suggests that this can also work in a negative dimension.

Resuming (informal) power-sharing talks post-1974

Negotiations to restore power-sharing were interrupted by the Turkish invasion of the island on 20 July 1974. Turkey intervened militarily to avert what it saw as an attempt by the Greek junta to unite Cyprus with Greece in a coup against President Makarios five days earlier. During the invasion, approximately 140,000 Greek Cypriots were forced by the Turkish military to flee from the North, while about 40,000 Turkish Cypriots living in the South chose (or were coerced) to abandon their houses and move to the North (Fisher 2001: 311). The Turkish invasion and resulting demographic changes have also necessitated new political understandings as to a renegotiated power-sharing. However, the prolonged conflict, the isolation of the two communities, and the displacement of more than one-third of the population have made the resumption of consociationalism more difficult.

Since 1974, UN proposals and resolutions for a negotiated settlement in Cyprus have stipulated new federal/territorial and consociational provisions. It has been generally assumed that a prospective negotiated settlement will incorporate two federal units and a shared administration at the central government level. Terms such as 'bizonal' and 'bicommunal' federation (BBF) used in Cyprus, as well as references to 'political equality' included in already agreed framework agreements by the leaders of the two communities, point to a general convergence on sharing power accepted by all sides, although, admittedly, the details and substance of a future settlement remain to be resolved.

Despite the overall failing peace process, the broader vision for a reunited federal Cyprus has often created incentives for successful informal cooperation on a number of issues. For instance, since the late 1970s current Turkish Cypriot leader Mustafa Akinci (then mayor of the Turkish Cypriot part of Nicosia) and his Greek Cypriot counterpart Lellos Demetriades resorted to an *ad hoc* set of arrangements to address the city's impending environmental disaster in the absence of a sewer system. The two leaders left formalities aside and even refrained from signing a contract at the time. Instead the two mayors agreed to call themselves *representatives* rather than *mayors* of the city and managed, through an informal collaboration, to upgrade the city's sewer system, making the first step to Nicosia's reunification. While both faced strong opposition from hardline leadership, particularly given the proximity of this achievement to the events of 1974, they pointed to expert advice to alert the public and elected officials of the imminent dangers of a looming environmental crisis facing the capital city.

At the high table, formal progress has also been made on multiple issues, though without the two Cypriot communities making it to the final point of a comprehensive settlement. For the most part, all the peace plans and packages proposed so far represent a compromise between the aspirations of different parties. Against the wishes of Turkish and Turkish Cypriot hardliners, the UN has attempted to re-establish Cyprus as a unified state with significant territorial readjustments in favor of the Greek Cypriot side to enable the maximum number of returnees among the post-1974 victims of ethnic cleansing. Against the wishes of Greek Cypriot hardliners, it adopted ethnic federal structures recognizing significant autonomy for the future Turkish Cypriot constituent state and political equality within the central government. UN proposals aimed to establish a form of power-sharing and designated community rights, thereby preventing the Greek Cypriot majority from out-voting Turkish Cypriots on issues of vital political concern. On the issue of security, the UN attempted in the summer of 2017 to abolish Greek and Turkish unilateral guarantees for intervention. However, significant disagreements remain as to the timing and conditions for the complete withdrawal of Turkish troops.

Despite intensive efforts to renegotiate new and comprehensive security, territorial and power-sharing arrangements, the island still remains divided. Unlike the other two main cases in this book, at the time of writing, Cyprus remains a failed case of consociational mediation. The Cyprus problem has therefore been described by many as the 'diplomat's graveyard', a 'term often used to describe the effect the intractable Cyprus issue has had on the parade of UN representatives who had tried to help fund a settlement, only to depart empty handed' (Christou, 2014). A book published to mark the UN's 50th anniversary on the island includes 25 envoys and eight secretary-generals who have contributed to the island's peace talks (Hadjigregoriou, 2014).

Yet an alternative view is to consider a number of successful outcomes from these mediations, particularly in humanitarian and confidence-building measures. Besides the example of Nicosia (and its now vibrant bicommunal culture), Cyprus has so far developed a number of proto-consociational structures with various projects, associations and committees currently operating against its long stalemate. These include, for instance, the Committee for Missing Persons, which is responsible for exhuming remains of the missing from the 1963–1974 violence (Kovras, 2017; Yakinthou, 2017): the Committee on Cultural Heritage for the restoration of ancient monuments including mosques, churches and monasteries; and committees on gender, education and crisis management (Makriyianni & Psaltis, 2007; Psaltis et al 2017).[2] In the past decade, historical monuments have been protected from destruction, police have prevented crimes (recently, a child abduction) and both sides have helped each other with regard to electricity shortages, most notably following the Mari explosion in 2011.

These technical committees as well as other successful bicommunal projects are by no means a substitute for a settlement. Yet, they have done significant and fairly independent work in their respective areas of expertise, despite calls by hardliners on both sides to interrupt or curtail their operations. Although they lack accountability (as representatives are not voted on, unlike, for instance, proposals for a constitutional convention), their major strength is that they rely on volunteer work and have so far addressed issues of primary importance for local communities including the relatives of victims, enclave communities and (potential) returnees, such as members of the Maronite community who were permitted to return under Turkish Cypriot administration. In fact, following the summer 2017 stalemate, both leaders have agreed to support their communities through confidence-building measures rather than engage in retaliatory acts. Such early, informal steps could create the conditions for a more formal arrangement on power-sharing and even a more dynamic type of 'living consociationalism' as described in the case of Brussels in the previous chapter.

What power-sharing? Past proposals and limitations

Power-sharing in Cyprus could take a number of different forms, each of which could be reflected in an electoral design or system of government – for instance, in a parliamentary or presidential democracy, or even in a semi-presidential system integrating the two. Before selecting one arrangement, however, it is important to summarise some broader criteria for power-sharing, as these are reflected in the discussions of other divided societies earlier in this book. First, power-sharing arrangements should carry the promise of functioning smoothly, even if elected hardliners veto important legislation in an attempt to challenge federal unity. Equally, if political parties from the divided communities fail to form a governing coalition (as, for instance, in Belgium during its record-breaking 541 days without an elected coalition government in 2010 and 2011), mechanisms to resolve deadlocks should be in place to ensure the proper functioning of the central government. Second, it is necessary to consider how a power-sharing proposal accommodates the interests of the disputing political parties, a crucial question in the current Cyprus peace talks. This is an essential aspect of any mediation, as individual parties are unlikely to endorse an electoral or governance system in the peace talks or subsequent referendums if any of its provisions threaten their basic interests and future capacity to serve their communities. Third, a power-sharing arrangement could formalise decision making in the most detailed fashion possible to preclude ambiguity.

So far, two main comprehensive policies have been proposed for Cyprus: a parliamentary system stipulated in the 2002–2004 Annan Plan and a presidential cross-voting arrangement agreed upon by Talat and Christofias in 2009 and revisited by Akinci and Anastasiades in the period 2015–2017. If the Annan Plan had been approved by Greek Cypriots in the 2004 referendum, the reunited island would have had a Senate with a 50–50 composition, reflecting the political equality of the constituent states (or rather the two communities), and a Chamber of Deputies, reflecting the majority Greek Cypriot population of the island (75% and 25% for Greek and Turkish Cypriots, respectively).

In all versions of the plan, ordinary decisions in the Senate would require a majority of the senators to agree, including at least a quarter of the representatives from each constituent state. On issues of vital interest, such as the election of the Presidential Council, there was a provision for a special majority of at least two-fifths of the senators from each side (UN, 2003, paragraph 86; UN, 2004a; 2004b). This 'double majority' procedure is not unusual for the power-sharing systems covered in previous chapters. Parliamentary vetoes have been employed, for instance, in a limited number of matters in the BCR parliament under the condition that an absolute majority of two-thirds from each language group oppose a specific legislation. In Brussels a spare solution exists on this issue as well; if a majority cannot be found in each language group (on the top of a majority in the BCR parliament overall), a second vote is organised at least 30 days later for which only one-third of the votes are necessary in each language group.

In theory, the Annan Plan drew on these precedents and sounded promising. However, in practice both communities on the island expressed reservations. Greek Cypriots feared that the strict bizonal character of the Senate would prevent decision-making in the Presidential Council because of the Turkish Cypriot veto. For their part, Turkish Cypriots feared potential deadlocks in the Greek Cypriot–dominated Chamber of Deputies. Interestingly, while maintaining the positive aspects of consociationalism, the 2004 UN plan had significantly watered down the 1960s Turkish Cypriot veto.

Depending on the issue, a coalition including 20–40%Turkish Cypriots was proposed as a compromise in the federal structures of reunited Cyprus (UN 2003:18; Loizides, 2014).

Meanwhile, the 'moderate' critics of the Annan Plan criticised its 'lack of integrative' elements. Several independent proposals at the time suggested possible improvements, including the concept of cross-voting between the two communities (Emerson & Tocci 2002; Rotberg 2003; Anastasakis et. al. 2004). Cross-voting or weighted voting has a long history on the island, and it is undeniably the most innovative idea produced in informal bicommunal workshops, particularly leftist-dominated ones, in recent decades, pointing to an early and vibrant federal culture in the island. Costa Carras and the London-based Friends of Cyprus association have lobbied for such arrangements since the late 1970s. References to cross-voting were included in the Greek Cypriot proposals of 1989 (ibid). During the Annan Plan talks, however, cross-voting was excluded because the Turkish Cypriot side argued during the negotiations that this electoral mechanism was incompatible with 'genuine' Turkish Cypriot representation. For their part, Greek Cypriots showed little interest, even though the National Council had advocated cross-voting proposals since 1989 (UN, 2003, paragraph 86; UN, 2004a; Loizides & Keskiner 2004).

Interestingly, the failure of the Annan Plan in 2004 (or rather the overwhelming vote against the UN proposal by the Greek Cypriot community) did not result in the strengthening of anti-deal forces in the island. As noted, both sides found themselves instead under pressure domestically and internationally to set up projects and technical committees to increase cooperation, bicommunal contact and mutual understanding. And by 2008, both communities had elected moderate leaders from the traditionally pro-settlement left.

In principle, the 2009 compromise on cross-voting by Turkish Cypriot leader Mehmet Ali Talat and Greek Cypriot leader Dimitris Christofias could have been a catalyst for bicommunal negotiations. Briefly stated, the 2009 compromise stipulated the following: it allowed all Cypriots a double vote, one in their ethnic community and another (with a suggested standardised weight of 20%) in the other community. In the presidential election, every person would have one vote, making Turkish Cypriots an electoral minority of around 20%. In a second election, Turkish Cypriots would vote for the co-president. Greek Cypriots would participate but with a weighted vote of about 20%. Thus, the Greek Cypriot vote would be significantly weighted, and the community would have an electoral minority of Turkish Cypriots. The Greek Cypriot president would be head of government two-thirds of the time; the Turkish Cypriot one-third of the time. In cases of constitutional deadlock, the acting president would have the winning vote and play the role of arbitrator.

Critics responded that weighted votes and rotating presidencies was a Cypriot innovation with no international precedents. Although, admittedly, no such system operates elsewhere, deviations from the 'one person, one vote' principle are very common in divided societies, particularly in federations. In previous work we demonstrate how, contrary to the Northern Ireland model, in Brussels the various mechanisms of minority protection have substantially modified proportional representation, resulting in what has been called a 'protective dis-proportional representation model' for Belgium's capital region (Bodson and Loizides, 2017).

By their very nature, federal systems try to balance individual rights with those of constituent federal units, drawing on weighted voting systems to do so. In Switzerland, for example, apart from the system of rotating presidency, 'one citizen from Uri outweighs 34 citizens from Zurich' (Linder 1994). Linder notes that in theory 9% of the Swiss population (those residing in the smallest cantons) can block a democratic majority of 91%(ibid).

Such ratios are not unique to Switzerland. In northern Italy, in the little-known case of South Tyrol, a German-speaking population of about 290,000 shares the space with an Italian-speaking population of 120,000 and 18,000 Ladins. A major feature of power-sharing in South Tyrol is the compulsory rotation of offices in the presidency of the provincial assembly. The presidency consists of one president and one vice-president who are elected by the assembly. In the first half of every five-year legislative period, a representative of the German-speaking group must be elected president and an Italian elected vice-president; in the second half, their roles reverse (Wolff, 2009:14–15). At another level of power-sharing, in the joint regional assembly of the provinces of South Tyrol and Trentino (forming the region of Trentino-Alto Adige/Südtirol), majority Italians and minority German-speakers rotate the presidency and vice-presidency.

Bosnia provides a third relevant example. Although devastated by the civil war, the country has entered a recovery stage and has recently begun the process of joining the European Union. Through power-sharing is guaranteed by the presence of international forces, the country escaped the trajectory of its past and did not follow other regional examples, such as, for instance, the informal partition of Kosovo. Bosnia has even now formed a united military, an unimaginable development a decade ago. Following the examples of Switzerland and South Tyrol, Bosnia has a presidency that rotates between a Croat, a Muslim and a Serb (Bieber 2006; Belloni 2008). In Republika Srpska, the candidate with the highest number of votes wins the race, whereas in the federation, the Bosniak (i.e. Bosnian Muslim) candidate and the Croat candidate with the highest number of votes win the election for state president. The 2000 demographic situation was Bosniaks 48%, Serbs 37.1%, and Croats 14.3%.[3] Thus, although Bosniaks outnumber Croats by four to one, the Bosniak and Croat presidents have almost equal influence. The Bosnian model is downplayed by Greek Cypriot elites, however, with socialist party EDEK even producing a documentary video in 2016 that misrepresented the impact of federalism in Bosnia to the Cypriot public.[4] Undoubtedly though, power-sharing in Bosnia has provided a political structure in the region that has helped to reduce violence and brought stability to a war-torn and hitherto partitioned country. Moreover, in post-war Bosnia, of the estimated 2.2 million people driven from their homes during the 1992–1995 war, an estimated 1,015,394 had returned by 2006. Even more interestingly, an impressive 457,194 have repatriated under minority status in areas administered by another ethnic group.[5]

The question that all of this points us to is why have all Cypriot proposals failed despite being supported by the United Nations and leading moderate parties in both communities? We suggest several possibilities. First, it is more difficult to establish power-sharing and political equality between Greek and Turkish Cypriots than between opponents in most other divided communities (e.g. Northern Ireland) because of the fundamental demographic inequality (historically Greek Cypriots have outnumbered Turkish Cypriots by four to one). If it is difficult for Ulster unionists, as noted in the Northern Ireland case, to accept political equality with the Irish nationalists (who are likely to outnumber them within a few decades), we can well imagine the reactions of the Greek Cypriot public. Also, continuing this particular comparison, the unionist majority over Irish nationalists has declined from a two-thirds/one-third balance to parity at the lower end of the age range, a demographic trend not mirrored in the case of Cyprus. It would be too crude to say that the unionist aversion to power-sharing evident in the 1970s dissipated over time in line with this demographic trend – but it certainly did not hurt to have greater balance across the two main ethnonational communities. An additional worry for the Greek Cypriots is the role of Turkey and Turkish settlers; the latter are often used to exaggerate fears that power-sharing will be a stepping stone for Turkish control of the entire island in the near future.

Moreover, unlike in the Brussels Capital Region (BCR), there are no immediate trade-offs for Greek Cypriots if they agree to endorse a compromise on power-sharing. In BCR (and South Tyrol), minority and majority positions alternate at different institutional levels. Dutch speakers are accommodated generously in the BCR, but they, in turn, accommodate French speakers as a minority within Belgium as a whole. Likewise, in Bosnia, the rotating presidency and federalism have not restricted displaced persons from regaining their property, residency or voting rights. Bosniaks (i.e. Bosnian Muslims) have compromised on national governance but gained an unrestricted right of return plus international guarantees for Dayton's implementation. Such 'incentives' are lacking for Greek Cypriots; instead, they are being asked to accept severe limits on the right of return for their own displaced persons under future Turkish Cypriot administrations and, in the best-case scenario, the 'incomplete withdrawal' of Turkish troops from the island following a peace settlement.

A general rethinking of these aspects of the Cyprus problem could suggest suitable incentives for a mutually agreed-upon power-sharing arrangement. It is also essential to revisit the power-sharing arrangements presented earlier in this book. What can be learned from other parliamentary systems in other divided societies, particularly those already operating within the European Union? And how can these lessons be applied to Cyprus? In the case of Cyprus, although everyone seems to agree that fresh ideas are needed, constructive out-of-the-box thinking has been blocked by expediency. Mediators are often rightly conservative in terms of their judgements of what will be accepted by the various sides, with parties at high-level talks avoiding mention of anything outside their comfort zone or immediate knowledge. We remain optimistic, however. The current stalemate, instead of being just another dead end, might open the door to new ways of thinking. We based this optimism on the development of an early peace culture in Cyprus, demonstrated in the examples of informal proto-consociationalism outlined above, which provides some traction for the development of a more formal comprehensive agreement in the near future.

How can Cyprus emerge from its stalemate?

Our set of prescriptions for Cyprus is fairly simple – three electoral systems could accommodate the interests of both Greek and Turkish Cypriots: a d'Hondt style following Northern Ireland's example, a Brussels Capital Region two-tier style arrangement and a system combining d'Hondt or Brussels with cross-voted presidents. Each could address the main concerns and build on the progress already made in negotiations of governance, first by Christofias and Talat and more recently by Anastasiades and Akinci. These potential options could be considered, taking into never several limitations of all three options. Under the right circumstances, Cyprus could be the first example of an ethnically partitioned society to reunify after four decades, with the mutual consent of majorities in referendums in both communities. For this to happen, peace mediators need new ideas that take into consideration the important precedents in similarly divided societies.

Option A: a Northern Ireland d'Hondt arrangement

In a d'Hondt cabinet or a similar method inspired by Northern Ireland, Cypriot political parties would automatically be entitled to ministerial positions by virtue of their representation in Parliament. They would be elected to these posts in Parliament through proportional representation. The Ministerial Council would be based on a ratio (for instance, 4GC to 2TC or 7GC to 4 TC) and there would be rotating first and second prime minister positions representing the two communities.

As noted in the first chapter, the d'Hondt executive is an innovation to power-sharing from Northern Ireland which entitles each political party to be proportionally represented in Parliament according to its total number of votes and to automatically translate its parliamentary representation into ministerial positions. The d'Hondt format is used in the allocation of parliamentary seats around the world, but its introduction in executive positions remains rare. Besides Northern Ireland, it is currently employed in the allocation of committee chairs in the European Parliament and in municipalities in Denmark – for example, in Copenhagen since 1938 (O'Leary et al. 2005). By inviting everyone to join the cabinet, d'Hondt or one of its variations could skip the most contentious aspect of consociationalism in divided societies, namely the forming of inter-ethnic majority coalitions. Northern Ireland operates through the principle of automaticity (McEvoy 2006; 2014). Party-nominated ministers' appointments cannot be vetoed by another party or parties; however, individual ministers themselves cannot exercise veto rights either. Double majorities from both denominations (i.e. communities) are required in the Northern Ireland assembly.

This inclusive power-sharing formula has multiple advantages, especially if matched with local political dynamics. For instance, using a power-sharing formula involving seven Greek Cypriots and four Turkish Cypriots might be the most suitable arrangement for the Cypriot context and would ensure broad representation as understood by local political actors. As mentioned earlier, such calculations offer the simplest and fairest way to share power in a society that is deeply divided, not only ethnically but also politically, between left and right. These formulas are based on the pragmatic assumption that a single party from each community cannot address the challenges of reunification. Broad d'Hondt-style coalitions allow everyone to participate in democratic governance without exclusions. This is particularly important as exclusionary power-sharing might turn significant constituencies against the peace settlement.

As suggested earlier, the automaticity of the formula eliminates the requirement of entering post-election negotiations to form a coalition (McEvoy 2006; 2014). Prolonged deadlocks in forming governments could be problematic during a global financial meltdown of the type seen in 2008 and in the economic crisis that followed. The absence of formal d'Hondt-style arrangements has left federal countries without elected governments for prolonged periods, as in Belgium in 2010 and 2011. Under d'Hondt, if parties do not voluntarily assume their assigned cabinet posts, others are entitled to step in. This is a major improvement from the parliamentary system of the Annan Plan, which sought the formation of coalitions similar to the Belgian national government model.

Option B: a Brussels Capital Region two-tier system

An alternative to d'Hondt is a system similar to Belgium's (or the Annan Plan) where parties negotiate cabinet formation and devise a program acceptable to concurrent majorities in both communities. This does not seem particularly applicable to Cyprus, however. Uniting under a common platform has obvious advantages in shaping policies, but there is no certainty that such coalitions will emerge given the long division of the island. Here the Brussels region's introduction of an innovative two-tier power-sharing system may be relevant in addressing this challenge for Cyprus. In the BCR plan, Dutch speakers and French speakers can agree to form a coalition representing concurrent majorities, but if they fail to do so, each community group appoints its own cabinet members by majority vote. As noted in the discussion of Brussels and Belgium in previous chapters, this default deadlock-resolving mechanism allows the executive to be appointed by political parties by each ethno-linguistic group separately, but only if they fail to form a cross-community coalition. The system compares positively to other, more formal arrangements that lack the flexibility needed in divided places. As we argued in Chapter 2, BCR's 'living consociationalism' allowed the region to adapt to circumstances and to transform itself from a symbol of confrontation between Dutch and French speakers into an oasis of stability and peace on the European continent.

The principle of automaticity is also present in the BCR model. As noted in Chapter 2, if the parties cannot agree on a distribution of the portfolios within the government, article 37 of the 1989 Brussels Act determines the competences of the five different ministries and describes the allocation process. According to this allocation mechanism, the minister-president is the first to choose which pre-determined competences he wants to exert; the two members of the French-speaking group are able to choose their preferred competences in the second and fourth position while the two ministers from the Dutch-speaking group choose the third and fifth position. Surprisingly, this spare mechanism has never been employed so far. The two community groups have managed to agree on a governing coalition following six elections (1989, 1995, 1999, 2004, 2009, 2014). In the current political context in BCR, it seems that using such spare solutions is symptomatic of a much-worsening relationship between community groups.

A key difference with Northern Ireland has been the size of the cabinet in the Brussels Capital Region. In Northern Ireland both the assembly and the cabinet were designed to provide broader inclusivity to major groups (and also to create incentive for their support to ending violence as well as committing their electorates to vote in favour of the Belfast/Good Friday Agreement in 2017). In the case of Brussels, one should note the limited number of portfolios (five, including the minister-president), which does make it impossible for all parties to take part in the governing coalition. In fact, most of the time only two or three parties can get a position in the government within each language group. Through the newly granted 'constitutive autonomy', the BCR parliament could decide to increase the number of portfolios within the government so that more parties could be included in the governing majority. Quite the contrary: since the 2017 snap elections, the oversized Northern Ireland Assembly has seen a reduction of its members from 108 to 90.

Switzerland offers another alternative whereby individual ministers have to gain parliamentary support, even though they are appointed by their own parties, with the informal understanding that all parties participate in government. As noted above, Switzerland's 'magic formula' (Linder 1994) enables each party to propose specific candidates to the Federal Council. Subsequently, they come under parliamentary scrutiny, and only those receiving support from the parliament can take up ministerial positions. This procedure facilitates the selection of broadly respected leaders and the exclusion of extremists on the far right (a concern in Cyprus with the rise of the Greek Cypriot far right party ELAM or in Brussels with the rise of Vlaams Belang).

The massive presence of members of the Vlaams Blok, a Flemish far right party, in the 1999–2004 legislature raised some concerns in the democratic parties that a further increase in the number of seats obtained by the Vlaams Blok would lead, first, to the impossibility to shape a government in the traditional way –through negotiations – and second, that the application of the spare solution would probably lead to the nomination of two ministers from the Vlaams Blok. Both cases constituted a risk for the institutional structure of BCR. Therefore, the democratic parties consented in the 2001 Lombard agreement to provide for another alternative 'spare solution' in case no majority could be found in the Dutch-speaking group specifically for the nomination of the ministers. The vote on the election of the Dutch-speaking minister would then be transferred to the Flemish Community Commission (FCC), which includes the 17 members of the Dutch-speaking group of BCR parliament plus five members coming from the Flemish parliament. These additional five members should make it possible to unlock the situation by contributing to the majority for the nomination of ministers (which would not include the Vlaams Blok).

Overall, the logic of the Swiss or BCR arrangement is that negotiated cross-community coalitions should not be prevented; although they are not a definite outcome, such options should be given a chance, at least in principle. Another consideration is broader inclusivity. Beyond social and ethnic divisions, any coalition could include gender quotas or quotas for vulnerable groups. For instance, if a party wins more than one seat in the cabinet, nominations should consider gender equality. Or special provisions could be introduced for (formerly) displaced persons aiming to preserve their rights in a reunited Cyprus.

Option C: combining d'Hondt or BCR models with cross-voted presidents

In our previous chapters, we acknowledge that the NI and the BCR models are not without flaws. On the issue of functionality, as we argued earlier in the book, a government of all parties as in d'Hondt could lack coordination, accountability and consensus. Northern Ireland can look to the UK and/or the Republic of Ireland for *ad hoc* arbitration, but Cyprus cannot rely on direct rule by Athens and/or Ankara if power-sharing arrangements fail. Alternative mechanisms have to be identified if parties use their cabinet posts to block important legislation or, worse yet, fail to enter a shared government. Disagreements might arise at different levels of governance within the cabinet, the parliaments or any sub-unit of the federation. The Annan Plan aimed at resolving such disputes through the arbitration of the Constitutional Court, but this would be a slow process at best.

While preserving these mechanisms, we suggest adding another layer of arbitration to the reunification structure by entrusting co-presidents with the authority to mediate future conflicts by consensus. When combined with a d'Hondt executive, co-presidential cross-voting would have many positive effects. In general, as we argue in the introduction, this mixed system combines a broad, inclusive 'Lijphartian' consociational d'Hondt cabinet with "Horowitzian" centripetalist cross-voting for a shared presidency, making it a much more feasible and effective alternative for Cyprus. For one thing, it would be more negotiable as both communities in Cyprus (and elsewhere) have often been governed by coalitions of moderates and hardliners. If the system were adopted, hardliners would be less likely to veto legislation, knowing that a co-president from their own community might reach a different compromise which would not necessarily reflect their preferences. Co-presidents would make decisions faster and in a more democratic fashion. They would have more flexibility in terms of time than the Constitutional Court and they would be able to negotiate linkages across different issues, thereby maximizing gains for the two communities. If a presidential deadlock occurred, it would be transferred to the Constitutional Court and ECHR judges (as in Bosnia).

The joint presidency would involve a cross-voting formula, as agreed upon by Christofias and Talat in 2009 and 2010. Executive power would lie primarily with the cabinet but the two co-presidents would maintain key arbitration powers and deal with certain critical issues, such as security and mediations with the United Nations force on the island. The most important responsibility of the co-presidents would be to mediate and arbitrate deadlocks at all levels of government. If there were remaining unresolved issues, community vetoes or protracted stalemates elsewhere in the system, the consensus of the two co-presidents would be sufficient to resolve disputes before the Constitutional Court or another arbitration mechanism was called upon. The presidential arbitration mechanism would add another democratic layer of governance to the reunification structure, creating a buffer zone between the Constitutional Court and the government. At the same time, it would soften objections to foreign arbitration, as two alternative deadlock-breaking mechanisms would be in place before such arbitration began.

If a semi-presidential arrangement were set up in Cyprus, it would be possible to define Turkish Cypriot leader Mustafa Akinci and Greek Cypriot leader Nicos Anastasiades (or his successor after the 2018 elections) as co-presidents, extending their terms and avoiding a lengthy co-presidential election. This would have multiple benefits. As the leaders who sign the settlement would be entrusted with deadlock-breaking duties, they could make a real difference in implementing an agreement in its first and most difficult years. That being said, continuing their terms in office would be more legitimate if their powers as co-president were largely symbolic and limited to arbitration. This provision would facilitate the transition to a united federal Cyprus, with the settlement gradually becoming implemented at various levels. Last but by no means least, establishing a co-presidency would increase the chances of winning a referendum given that leaders themselves would offer their guarantees and charisma to ensure that no deadlocks will derail the process of federalizing Cyprus.

Citizen preferences, referendums and a constitutional convention

While all these three options might sound attractive, a facilitating process to mediate a formal power-sharing arrangement in Cyprus is still missing. For comparative purposes, there has been no other ethnically partitioned society to reunify after four decades as currently attempted in Cyprus either through a presidential or a parliamentary system. Moreover, the fact that the two sides have agreed to seek the mutual consent of majorities in simultaneous referendums makes the negotiation process even more difficult. So far, very few formal referendums have been employed in related conflict mediation episodes and, of those, most have failed (Qvortrup 2013; Loizides 2014). As Colombia, Brexit and other contemporary cases suggest, referendums have a terrible track record in solving complex problems. In Cyprus, the two sides will need to consider not only the new institutional options presented above but also a fairly novel mediation and ratification process. Our cases from Brussels and Northern Ireland suggest a number of alternatives for divided societies not previously taken into consideration in policy debates. Besides peace referendums, these alternative options include widely inclusive multi-party talks (Northern Ireland) and constitutional conventions or special acts/ordinances (Brussels/Belgium).

Although now part of the conventional wisdom in Cyprus, it is not very clear how the idea of a referendum emerged in the island's protracted negotiations. As noted above, the Annan Plan included a process of twin referendums leading in 2004 to a *yes* vote in the Turkish Cypriot community and a *no* vote in the Greek Cypriot community. However, this idea had emerged in Cyprus decades before. As early as the 1980s, hardline Turkish Cypriot leader Rauf Denktash clearly outsmarted moderates on both sides by committing the two communities into this specific 'democratic' ratification process. Referendums are now taken for granted in the Cyprus peace talks, although there has been no legal or constitutional provision enabling such thinking.

Interestingly, this book's main cases utilized here to inspire the Cypriot negotiators have taken opposite sides on referendums. On the one hand, the island of Ireland has relied heavily on direct democracy (like Switzerland) and could provide useful lessons in the general management of a future referendum particularly on technical issues and general guidelines. Northern Ireland itself voted in 1998 for the Good Friday Agreement (while the republic held a simultaneous vote in the South) but only after an inclusive all-party mediation process also leading to the d'Hondt system (see also Amaral, forthcoming). Brussels, on the other hand, did not employ referendums as an instrument of popular ratification. Belgium itself has an unfortunate experience with consultations. Indeed, despite the fact that referendums and consultations at the national level are unconstitutional in Belgium, a plebiscite was organised in 1950 on the question of the return of King Leopold III to Belgium. The consultation bitterly divided the two community groups and threatened the unity of the country (Qvortrup, 2002:22).

Instead, mediation in the Brussels Capital Region took place through a special ordonnance (adopted in the BCR parliament), through a constitutional reform or, alternatively, the adoption of a special act (in the federal parliament). A constitutional convention on major issues requires the multiple steps described in Chapter 2, specifically a decision from the parliament as to which provisions to change, an election for a new parliament and the decision of newly elected representatives to go ahead and finally to present the proposals for ratification by a two-thirds majority.

In Cyprus, relying simply on a referendum for ratification could prove extremely difficult given the experience of other divided societies, highly polarizing throughout the mediation process, and arguably unfair to certain groups disproportionately affected by the settlement (e.g. property owners). At the more practical level, a lesson from the 2016 and 2017 mediations is that referedum provisions might obstruct sides from making concesssions in the first place. In a meeting with the second author, the UN Secretary-General Special Envoy in Cyprus revealed privately that during the peace talks, leaders repeatedly rejected compromises, citing their public opinion and impact on a future referendum.[6]

Cypriot mediators have not only opted for a difficult ratification process through a referendum but have also failed to consider available alternatives. Given that now is taken for granted, it might be wise at the minimum to combine a referendum with other informal consultation processes involving political parties, civil society actors and those who will be most affected by the settlement (e.g. refugees/property owners). The format of two Cypriot leaders negotiating in (selective) secrecy has been failing for decades. Images of foreign leaders deciding on the future of Cyprus in a distant Swiss resort do not seem to resonate very well with the public.

To cover this gap, our cases suggest alternative ways to go forward. It has been common in other comparable conflicts to include major political parties in the mediations. In the Cyprus case this could be tied to negotiating on the basis of the 2017 Guterres package replicating the format and principles Senator Mitchell introduced in Northern Ireland. As parties have a commitment on referendums for decades now, the settlement will still need to win public endorsement. But there might be space for adding new components to the existing agreement – for instance, a gradual ratification process first by the people in a mandate referendum and then relying on a constitutional convention or an implementing body to be created as an ad hoc ratification mechanism to support the two leaders.

Admittedly, constitutional conventions by their very name imply a formalised arrangement. Such arrangements in the form of constitutional conventions are difficult to achieve, because sides have to agree on power-sharing, security and other federal issues in advance. Constitutional conventions require governments, opposition and civil society groups to work together, therefore their emergence will require major investment in time and effort. For example, in the case of Cyprus, Auer (2009:21) proposed the creation of an elected body of around 100 representatives 'permitting a broad representation of the most significant of the political entities and civil societies of Cyprus'. Such formal arrangements tend to receive attention from spoilers and alienate undecided voters as demonstrated in the 'grandiose vision' of replacing existing treaties with a formal constitution for the European Union. On the contrary, upgrading the current technical committees could offer leaders less vulnerable alternatives in the negotiations.

There are also lessons here not to be learnt from Northern Ireland and the BCR models. A key difference in Cyprus relates to the fact that voters have different stakes in a settlement. Displaced persons willing to return to their properties or be compensated have a different profile towards the settlement compared to the rest of the population; in fact, in a related survey among Greek Cypriots we demonstrated that it is very likely that a non-IDP vote might prevent the settlement despite support by displaced persons (Psaltis et al. 2016). To address this gap, an alternative process could focus on displaced persons in compliance with the UN recommendations on property restitution (Pinheiro principles, particularly paragraph 14, emphasising prior consultation with owners and users).[7] A comprehensive census of those whose property rights will be affected by the settlement could be a game changer for the peace talks in Cyprus. There are plenty of technical solutions available to help sides identify amicable compromises before resorting to arbitrary and hard-to-mediate provisions. It would also allow the matching of preferences on specific properties, thus largely avoiding the very difficult, possibly unresolvable, question of who has priority by making clear arrangements that are binding, generous and acceptable to at least the overwhelming majority of individual owners/users. This type of democratic, accountable and detailed technical preparation has been missing so far in Cyprus. Presumably, it will be set up anyway as a first step if a settlement is ever reached. However, introducing it earlier rather than later will allow displaced persons to be consulted early enough and identify acceptable solutions for each individual – a necessary step for maximising public support and inclusivity in both communities.

Conclusion

An inclusive political system in a federal Cyprus would enable moderate parties to cooperate without alienating hardliners or upsetting coalition preferences among political parties for government or municipal posts. By relying on a pure presidential system with or without cross-voting, a moderate party might face two equally problematic situations: being excluded from future coalitions or running the government alone against united opposition, including its own community. By extension, parties would risk losing critical allies or being outflanked. For example, in the Greek Cypriot community, if moderate leftist AKEL forms a joint campaign together with Turkish Cypriot parties, the moderate centre-right DISY would align with hardliner DIKO and EDEK to exclude AKEL from federal, state and municipal posts, and vice versa.

In contrast, d'Hondt-style arrangements eliminate the fear of exclusion and minimise political risks for all actors, enabling constructive collaborations. Moreover, because d'Hondt-style executives do not distinguish between hardliners and moderates, all parties receive a fair proportional representation in government. Once in cabinet, moderates and hardliners have the same incentives to compromise by trading on issues that are less important in exchange for issues that are absolute priorities. Advocates of d'Hondt argue that engaging hardliners in compromises whilst they are in power is preferable to having them obstruct the peace process in opposition. As noted in previous chapters, the Northern Ireland experience demonstrates that when hardliners increase their support, they do so by substantially moderating their agendas on critical issues.

To negotiate the most favourable electoral system for an aspiring federation or consociation, a set of additional interrelated conditions must be considered early in the process. The most critical of these conditions is the provision of multiple mechanisms to address deadlocks if one side decides to veto key legislation. As we noted in our recommendations above, a semi-presidential system would mean that either consensus at any level, at the parliament (i.e. cabinet) or cross-voted presidency level, or even a third arbitration by a constitutional court or an external body/wise persons committee, would be sufficient to resolve a dispute. Such a system would capitalise on the specific advantages of Cyprus as a federation. First, it would be more negotiable and acceptable to all parties. Second, the formula would combine the broader participation of Turkish Cypriot political forces maintaining the community's veto with an alternative arbitration mechanism fostering cooperation. With a two-tier BCR-style model, for instance, new negotiated coalitions would be likely to emerge, adding functionality and a decisive orientation to the possibility of a reunited Cyprus.

Any of the three options proposed here would allow the broader participation of Greek Cypriot political parties, specifically facilitating minimum cooperation from the two rival parties in the Greek Cypriot community: the right-wing DISY and communist AKEL. This would safeguard a settlement, as both parties are predominantly moderate in their pro-settlement attitudes. This advantage is not unique in Cyprus, and as we argue in the conclusion, could address similar dynamics in Lebanon, Syria or Sri Lanka, as well as other cases in divided societies.

Fostering consensus is a formidable task in post-conflict societies, but it arguably becomes manageable if societies overcome legitimate fears and embrace available institutional innovations. Power-sharing arrangements have been successfully negotiated and implemented, even amidst heightened inter-communal mistrust. By departing from the winner-take-all logic, power-sharing allows societies to embrace novel understandings of public engagement, whereby the more parties share power, the better the prospects are for effective and sustainable management. Also, as the Northern Ireland case has demonstrated (especially between 2007 and 2017), the practicalities of sharing power in divided societies can usefully bring socio-economic issues and resource allocation into the foreground. This does not of itself resolve lingering ethnonational tensions, but it does at least supplement them with day-to-day mechanics of governance and provide evidence of the capacity of political opponents to co-operate in their joint interests.

Beyond peace and stability for post-conflict societies, consensus democracies have several other advantages: facilitating decision making, increasing the durability of policies and strengthening grass-roots support, while allowing the moderation of anti-systemic elements. As noted above, Cyprus has already developed proto-consociational structures in many areas that may be able to set a positive tone for reunification. Despite the challenges ahead, Cyprus could indeed be the first example of an ethnically partitioned society to reunify, despite a *de facto* separation of more than four decades.

Notes

1 Such feelings of insecurity continue to be very strong for both communities. Threats and how those are framed in public discourse, as in the case of Northern Ireland, can be very powerful as well. When in February 2017 the parliament voted to commemorate the 1950 *enosis* plebiscite in which 96% of Greek Cypriots voted for union with Greece, Turkish Cypriots left the power-sharing talks while (perceived) failures to address the existential fears of Greek Cypriots led to the collapse of the talks in the summer of 2017.
2 For a full list see https://kktcb.org/en/technical-committees
3 www.cia.gov/library/publications/the-world-factbook/geos/bk.html
4 www.youtube.com/watch?v=jKWzLO0MCLU
5 Updated numbers can be found at the UNHCR Bosnia website: http://www.unhcr.org/bosnia-and-herzegovina.html
6 Personal communication with UN Special Envoy Espen Barth Eide, October 26, 2016, Nicosia.
7 https://2001-2009.state.gov/documents/organization/99774.pdf

Bibliography

Adams, T. W. (1966) 'The First Republic of Cyprus: A Review of an Unworkable Constitution.' *The Western Political Quarterly* 19 (3): 475–490.
Amaral J. (forthcoming 2017) 'Elite Mediation and the Cypriot Communities' Support for the Annan Plan' *Cooperation and Conflict*.

Anastasakis, O., Gilles, B., & Kalypso, N. (2004) 'Getting to Yes: Suggestions for Embellishment of the Annan Plan for Cyprus.' *South East European Studies Programme (SEESP)*, February. www.sant.ox.ac.uk/areastudies/Oxford_Cyprus.pdf

Anderson, P. (2008) 'The Divisions of Cyprus.' *London Review of Books* 30 (8): 7–16 (available online at www.lrb.co.uk/v30/n08/perry-anderson/the-divisions-of-cyprus)

Andreas A. (2009) 'On the Way to a Constitutional Convention for Cyprus' in Auer A. & Triga, V. (eds.), *The Constitutional Convention for Cyprus*, Wissenschaftlicher Verlag Berlin, pp. 13–27, p. 21.

Attalides, M. (1977) 'The Turkish Cypriots: Their Relations to the Greek Cypriots in Perspective.' in Attalides, M. (ed.), *Cyprus Reviewed*. Nicosia: The Jus Cypri Association, pp. 71–101.

Bahcheli, T. (1972) *Communal Discord and the State of Interested Governments in Cyprus, 1955–70*, Doctoral Thesis, University of London.

Belloni, R. (2008) *State Building and International Intervention in Bosnia*, London: Routledge.

Bieber, F. (2006) *Post-War Bosnia: Ethnicity, Inequality and Public Sector Governance*, New York: Palgrave Macmillan.

Bodson, T. and Loizides, N. (2017). 'Consociationalism in the Brussels Capital Region: Dis-Proportional Representation and the Accommodation of National Minorities'. in: McCulloch, A. and McGarry, J. eds. *Power-Sharing: Empirical and Normative Challenges*. Routledge

Christou, J. (2014) *Exhuming the Diplomats Graveyard Cyprus Mail*. http://cyprus-mail.com/2014/05/11/exhuming-the-diplomats-graveyard/

Demetriou, C. (2012) 'Political Radicalization and Political Violence in Palestine, Ireland and Cyprus.' *Social Science History*, 36 (3): 391–420.

Emerson, M., & Tocci, N. (2002) *Cyprus as Lighthouse of the East Mediterranean: Shaping EU Accession and Re-unification Together*, Brussels: Centre for European Policy Studies.

Ertekün, M. Necati. (1981) *The Cyprus Dispute and the Birth of the Turkish Republic of Northern Cyprus*, Northern Cyprus: K. Rustem & Brother.

Fisher, R. (2001) 'Cyprus: The Failure of Mediation and the Escalation of an Identity-Based Conflict to an Adversarial Impasse.' *Journal of Peace Research* 38 (3): 307–326.

Hadjigregoriou, S. (2014). *The Facilitators. The UN Representatives & Advisers to Cyprus, 1964–2014*, MAM Publishers, Nicosia.

Joseph, J. (1997) *Cyprus: Ethnic Conflict and International Politics: From Independence to the Threshold of the European Union*, New York: St. Martin's Press.

Ker-Lindsay, J. (2004) *Britain and the Cyprus Crisis, 1963–1964*. No. 27. Bibliopolis.

Kovras, I. (2017) *Grassroots Activism and the Evolution of Transitional Justice: The Families of the Disappeared*, Cambridge University Press, Cambridge.

Lijphart, A. (1968) *The Politics of Accommodation: Pluralism and Democracy in the Netherlands*, University of California Press, Berkeley.

Lijphart, A. (1977) *Democracy in Plural Societies: A Comparative Exploration*, Yale University Press, New Haven.

Lijphart, A. (1994) *Electoral Systems and Party Systems (A Study of Twenty-Seven Democracies 1945–1990*, Oxford University Press, Oxford.

Lijphart, A. (2004) 'Constitutional Design for Divided Societies.' *Journal of Democracy* 15 (2): 96–109.

Linder, W. (1994) *Swiss Democracy: Possible Solutions to Conflict in Multicultural Societies*, St. Martin's Press, London.

Linz, J. J. (1990) 'The Perils of presidentialism.' *Journal of Democracy* 1 (1): 51–69.

Loizides, N. (2014) 'Negotiated Settlements and Peace Referendums.' *European Journal of Political Research* 53 (2): 234–249.

Loizides, N. & Keskiner, E. (2004) "The Aftermath of the Annan Plan Referendums: Cross-Voting Moderation for Cyprus". *Southeast European Politics*, V (2–3): 158–171.

Makriyianni, C, & Psaltis. C. "The teaching of history and reconciliation." *Cyprus Review* – 19.1 (2007): 43.

McEvoy, J. (2006) 'The Institutional Design of Executive Formation in Northern Ireland.' *Regional and Federal Studies* 16 (4): 447–464.

McEvoy, J. (2014) *Power-Sharing Executives: Governing in Bosnia, Macedonia and Northern Ireland*, University of Pennsylvania Press, Philadelphia.

McGarry, J. (2011) 'Centripetal Theory and the Cyprus Conflict,' paper presented at the *Workshop on Power-Sharing*, organized by the Ethnicity and Democratic Governance Project, Munk Centre, University of Toronto, 17 November.

McGarry, J. (2017) 'Centripetalism, Consociationalism and Cyprus: The "Adoptability" Question.' *Political Studies* 65(2): 512–529.

McGarry, J., & Loizides, N. (2015) 'Power-Sharing in a Re-United Cyprus: Centripetal Coalitions vs. Proportional Sequential Coalitions.' *International Journal of Constitutional Law* 13(4): 847–872.

McGarry, J., & O'Leary, B. (2009) 'Power Shared after the Deaths of Thousands' in Taylor, R. (ed.), *Consociational Theory: McGarry and O'Leary and the Northern Ireland Conflict*, Routledge, London, pp. 15–85.

Necatigil, Z. (1989) *The Cyprus Question and the Turkish Position in International Law*, Oxford University Press, Oxford.

O'Leary, B., Grofman, B., & Elklit, J. (2005) 'Divisor Methods for Sequential Portfolio Allocation in Multi-Party Executive Bodies: Evidence from Northern Ireland and Denmark).' *American Journal of Political Science* 49 (1): 198–211.

Papadakis, Y. (1999) 'Enosis and Turkish Expansionism: Real Myths or Mythical Realities?' in V. Calotychos (ed.), *Cyprus and Its People: Nation, Identity, and Experience in an Unimaginable Community, 1955–1997*. Boulder, CO: Westview Press, pp. 69–84.

Polyviou, P. G. (1980) *Cyprus, conflict and negotiation, 1960–1980*. Duckworth.

Psaltis, C., Carretero, M. & Čehajić-Clancy, S. "Conflict Transformation and History Teaching: Social Psychological Theory and Its Contributions." *History Education and Conflict Transformation*. Palgrave Macmillan, Cham, 2017. 1–34.

Psaltis C., Loizides, N. and Stefanovic, D. (2016) Views of Greek Cypriot Displaced Persons on Return and Referendum Vote, Presentation for the Directorate of Political Affairs, Council of Europe, Budapest June 29-July1.

Qvortrup, M. (2002) *A Comparative Study of Referendums (Government by the People)*, Manchester: Manchester University Press.

Qvortrup, M. (2013) *Balloting to Stop Bullets? Referendums and Ethnic Conflict*, University of Pennsylvania Press, Philadelphia, PA.

Rotberg, R. (2003) 'Cyprus After the Annan Plan: Next Steps Toward a Solution,' World Peace Foundation, Cambridge, MA.

Trimikliniotis, N. (2009) 'Pro: Rethinking the Un-viability of the Constitutional Arrangement.' in *Reunifying Cyprus: The Annan Plan and Beyond*, IB Tauris & Co Ltd, London, pp. 107–121.

UN. 2003. Document S/2003/398. Report of the Secretary-General on His Mission of Good Offices in Cyprus, April 1 <www.un.dk/doc/S.2003.398.pdf > [Accessed 19 January 2005]..

UN. 2004a. Document. *The Comprehensive Settlement of the Cyprus Problem, 31 March*. March 31, 2004 <www.cyprus-un-plan.org/Annan_Plan_Text1.html> [Accessed 19 January 2005]

UN. 2004b. "Document S/2004/43." *Report of the Secretary-General on his Mission of Good Offices in Cyprus*.

Wolff, S. (2009) "Complex Power Sharing as Conflict Resolution: South Tyrol in Comparative Perspective" (Available at www.stefanwolff.com/working-papers/STCPS.pdf accessed November 10 2010).

Xydis, S. G. (1973) *Cyprus: Reluctant Republic*. Vol. 11. The Hague: Mouton.

Yakinthou, C. (2017) 'Transitional Justice in Cyprus.' *Berghof Foundation*

Conclusion

In this book, we have examined a set of relatively under-studied empirical and conceptual innovations in consociational theory and practice, drawing specifically on two relative success stories, those of Northern Ireland and the Brussels Capital Region, and applying our findings to the case of Cyprus and beyond. Although all of our cases are problematic, each offers sophisticated and original ideas for national, regional and urban governance. In this conclusion, we draw out the broader contributions of our work to consociational theory and practice. We then explore the wider applicability of our findings, building on examples from the Middle East and elsewhere, with an emphasis on initiating a debate on post-conflict scenarios for Syria. We demonstrate how our comparison of Brussels, Northern Ireland and Cyprus provides a wide range of evidence-based prescriptions for emerging consociations and federations, as well as conflict mediations across the world.

Contributions of the work to theory and practice

In this book, we deal extensively with one of the key dichotomies in the study of power-sharing, specifically the tensions between those scholars supporting consociational approaches and those supporting centripetalist ones. Taking exception to much of the current literature, we suggest the potential for a symbiotic rather than an adversarial relationship between these scholarships. As noted in our introductory chapter, advocates of consociationalism argue for guaranteed group representation, such as minority veto rights and ethnic federalism, whereas elites come together to govern in the interests of society because they recognise the dangers of non-cooperation (Lijphart 2004; McGarry & O'Leary, 2007). Meanwhile, centripetalists advocate limits on group rights and argue for incentives for cross-community cooperation, aiming to foster consensus by integrating voting across moderates (Horowitz, 1985, 2013; Reilly, 2012). Instead of building in mutual vetos for groups, the centripetal approach seeks to generate individual moderation through the electoral system, where integrative behaviour gradually replaces ethno-national separation from the grass roots and upwards into the political elites. Unsuprisingly, the consociational and centripetalist schools appear to be polar opposites, as they offer radically different interpretations, causal remedies and prescriptions. Yet our three cases suggest that there is more space for complementarity and synthesis than is commonly assumed.

In the case of Brussels, the coexistence of two language groups has largely influenced the organization of the BCR institutions. Mechanisms unique to the consociationalist approach have indeed proliferated within the parliamentary and governmental structures. The separation of the BCR parliament into two language groups, the allocation of a fixed number of seats to each of these groups, the parity rule within the government and the other mechanisms protecting the Dutch-speaking minority make the BCR a consociational model in which the ethno-linguistic groups are forcefully affirmed. Interestingly, these protection mechanisms often entail co-decision proceedings and thus a kind of veto power for both community groups. This has resulted in a rather successful form of cooperation of both ethno-linguistic groups in Brussels and indeed in a smooth co-administration of the region. In other words, the minority protection mechanisms, which are typical for the consociationalist approach, promote in the BCR positive incentives for inter-ethnic cooperation and encourage political moderation. As such, these measures not only acknowledge the co-existence of several community groups but also require a strong cooperation between them – a cooperation that invites community groups to go beyond their differences. This goal is, in turn, typical for the centripetalist approach. Other mechanisms further indicate an attempt to transcend the separation into language groups in the BCR. For instance, voters in Brussels can decide on the day of the election to vote for lists belonging to the FSG or to the DSG. Therefore, they are not constrained to a specific language group. Political parties regularly take advantage of this situation by 'electoral shopping' in the other community group. Furthermore, in the case of Brussels, we identify a two-tier power-sharing system, where an effort is made to integrate alternative interests through a coalition of moderates who have reached a programmatic agreement on governance (i.e. employing a centripetalist device favouring moderation). If the integration of alternative inter-ethnic interests fails, however, the Brussels structure has a default solution, where majorities in each group allow for the appointment of cabinet ministers independently (i.e. employing a consociational approach accommodating ethnic interests). The consociationalist and centripetalist approaches are thus often interlinked in BCR.

Likewise, the case of Northern Ireland suggests a fairly flexible system, where voters are confronted with a liberal form of consociationalism. Unlike classic consociational approaches, in the d'Hondt system, the citizens of Northern Ireland are not forced to enter a separate ethnic electoral roll based on their ethnicity or vote solely for candidates representing their group. Instead, they can choose to vote for any candidate or party. If a democratic choice is made for moderate candidates at the centre, Northern Ireland will come closer to fulfilling the predictions of the centripetalist school, but if the current predominantly ethnic voting patterns persist, it will continue to function (or fail to do so) in a consociational way. It could also be argued that the liberal consociational system that has operated in Northern Ireland since 1999 has had a centripetalist dimension in producing incentives for ethnonational moderation. Both of the main ethnonationalist parties, the Democratic Unionist Party (DUP) and Sinn Fein (SF), have grown significantly during this period, in part because they made policy changes that moved them into more centrist positions. The DUP were initially opposed to the 1998 Belfast/Good Friday Agreement reached in 1998 and campaigned against it in the subsequent referendum and assembly elections. DUP candidates first took their seats in office on the basis that this would be a better means of making the consociational institutions untenable. It then gradually moved to a position where it saw an opportunity for co-operation with a moderating nationalist party. For its part, SF moved from an initially radical militant position to one where they supported the timing of total weapons decommissioning by the Provisional IRA, and unambiguous support for a reformed policing service and the wider criminal justice system. While there was not an integrative dynamic evident here, the liberal consociational system of government in NI did illustrate the capacity of the institutions to provide incentives for political moderation, characteristic of the centripetalist approach.

The evolution of the consociational model in the Northern Ireland context also displays some centripetalist traits. In particular the move from government *without* opposition, to government *with* opposition, is significant. During the 2016–2017 assembly mandate (until the resignation of former deputy First Minister Martin McGuinness in January 2017) a number of opposition parties emerged within the political system. Some of these were formally recognised (UUP and SDLP); other, smaller opposition factions were not. The important point to note is that the liberal consociational rules governing community designation and proportionality did not apply to the opposition parties. It was up to the UUP and SDLP to co-operate (or not), and this new system did not recognise or accommodate ethnonational rights or vetoes along the Unionist-Nationalist divide. It would be reasonable to say that during the relatively short period that this mandate was in existence, there was an informal non-aggression pact between the UUP and SDLP in opposition, and co-operation on an issue-by-issue basis. They did not demonstrate a capacity to work together as a joint opposition team, however, or to develop longer-term policy prospects across a range of issues that might allow them to present themselves as an alternative to the DUP/SF governing coalition. While this might have emerged over time had the assembly mandate lasted longer than eight months, it notably provides an example of a power-sharing system where the formal consociational principles had evolved over time to incorporate more centripetalist aspects – with an opposition that did not operate by the recognition of group rights and which could, if it wanted to, form an opposition coalition that would transcend the ethnonational divide between Unionism and Nationalism.

Lessons for the United Kingdom and Brexit

The main strength of the Brussels and Northern Ireland consociational systems is their capacity to adjust and provide attractive alternatives during the mediation and implementation phases of contested power-sharing agreements. Overall, both models offer the high degree of flexibility and adaptability required to meet the complex needs of contemporary societies. The case of Northern Ireland suggests that inclusive power-sharing arrangements could perform even within majoritarian (or centripetalist) systems. Following the Brexit referendum shock and calls for devolution throughout the United Kingdom, applying the Northern Ireland system to other parts of the UK could prove beneficial, particularly in urban governance. Currently the United Kingdom is one of the most centralised states in Europe, with increasing local demands for devolution following Brexit and the potential repatriation of powers from Brussels to London (as well as local administrations). Practitioners and policy actors working in this area should consider in advance a wide range of regional power-sharing models.

The literature has so far exclusively concentrated on the national level, but our selection of case studies opens up a whole new research area at the municipal and regional levels. The experience of post-conflict societies, particularly in the Balkans, has also shown municipalities to be effective local institutions in managing ethnic conflict (Koneska 2012) while in Northern Ireland municipal power-sharing in cities such as Derry/Londonderry preceded the 1998 Good Friday Agreement. The rationale for this early power-sharing was that consociationalism had to be equally exercised at different levels and that Ulster Unionists had to also be accommodated as a minority.[1] This within-case learning could be important for the United Kingdom, particularly for those groups campaigning for proportional representation (e.g. Make Votes Matter). By demonstrating the effectiveness of consensual institutions at the local or regional level, a much broader case could be made for political reform across the country.

It is worth mentioning that besides Brussels, Danish cities were employing similar power-sharing models even before the Second World War (O'Leary et al. 2005). While Scotland and Northern Ireland clearly voted to remain in the EU in the 2016 referendum on UK membership, their status as devolved regions of the UK gave some territorial definition and political significance to their respective results. In the context of NI's power-sharing system and the GFA that underpins it, the Brexit referendum led to some debate about whether the 'consent' principle at the heart of the GFA should also be extended to the UK's exit from the EU. Of course London also voted to remain – but its lack of distinct political autonomy in comparison to Scotland or NI made it more difficult to argue for self-determination or any form of opt-out over the Brexit process. Nonetheless, London's opposition to Brexit might create the impetus for a Brussels-style capital region as part of the broader restructuring of British politics and the need to maintain London's position as a global financial center.

Moreover, broader lessons from Northern Ireland are also important for British foreign policy and peace mediations assisted by the UK in the rest of the world. Besides Cyprus, where the United Kingdom is implicated directly through its guarantor status and the sovereign bases, NI's institutional lessons have been recommended in places of critical UK involvement such as Iraq (McGarry and O'Leary, 2007) and Colombia (Medina and Loizides, 2013). While our analysis recognises the limitations of these parallels, we remain optimistic overall over the future of power-sharing in Northern Ireland itself and the lessons it can inspire around the world. The province continues to progress as a society despite unprecedented shocks, most recently the triple effect of its own power-sharing failures, the Brexit referendum potentially undermining the GFA and reinstituting a hard border with the Irish Republic and the inconclusive 2017 election that saw the Conservative government relying on the Democratic Unionist Party (DUP) to stay in power.

Revisiting presidential consociations

In an effort to further challenge the centripetalist/consociational dichotomy, we have also explored a set of alternative designs for presidential consociations. For instance, our main recommendations for Cyprus in Chapter 3 draw on the d'Hondt process in the formation of an all-party cabinet, a Northern Ireland innovation also employed in different forms in Switzerland and elsewhere. Going beyond the Northern Ireland example *per se*, we add a variety of integrative elements to our proposals for Cyprus.

Specifically, we propose a mixed semi-presidential system for the Cypriot mediations, one combining a broad, inclusive 'Lijphartian' consociational cabinet with a 'Horowitzian' centripetalist cross-voted presidency. For one thing, a system that is broadly neutral and inclusive of all political parties would be more negotiable and durable in a divided society. For another, Northern Ireland's past and recent deadlocks suggest that effective arbitration mechanisms might be critically important. Among our major critiques of the Northern Ireland d'Hondt in Chapter 1 is that a government of all parties will likely lack coordination and consensus. D'Hondt works well as a mechanism to assist the swift formation of a governing Executive, but it is much less adept at promoting a sense of joint purpose among those who are appointed to office.

While the Annan Plan for Cyprus aimed at resolving such disputes through the arbitration of the Constitutional Court, this could lead to an unaccountable undemocratic form of governance. Moreover, the experience of the 2004 referendum suggests that it is hard to mediate such arrangements, as some of the parties might not welcome or trust foreign judges.

To address this issue, in Chapter 3, we propose adding another layer of arbitration in the Cypriot reunification structure, by investing cross-voted presidents with the authority to mediate future conflicts by consensus. In other words, we suggest a semi-presidential system with limited arbitration powers as agreed upon by the two Cypriot leftist leaders in 2009. The possible advantages of such an arrangement are twofold. Firstly, a semi-presidential arrangement might be easier to mediate. Turkish Cypriots are quite familiar with a semi-presidential systems because one is currently employed in their community. Likewise, Greek Cypriots might accept a new institutional arrangement more easily, as parliamentary or semi-presidential systems are more common in the European Union (currently Cyprus stands as an exception as the only purely presidential system in the EU). Secondly, semi-presidentialism would entice the support of the left for a future compromise without alienating either the right or political forces lacking contacts across the divide. This highly inclusive formula would address some of the fears of those skeptical about the settlement. At the same time, it could provide a functional power-sharing formula acceptable to Cyprus's reluctant 'moderates', who include both left and right.

A semi-presidential system may be able to overcome another key dilemma of divided societies – choosing between a parliamentary and a presidential system. In its summer 2017 mediation attempts in Cyprus, the UN (and the two sides) narrowed their options to a purely presidential system based on the 2009 Christofias-Talat agreement, despite a plethora of historical and contemporary evidence against presidentialism. Interestingly, the decision also went against the advice of the UN's own key expert on power-sharing;

more specifically, the latter argued that presidential arrangements would be more difficult to mediate (McGarry, 2017; and see also McGarry & Loizides, 2015). And, in fact, the mere prospect of a rotating presidency with strong executive powers proved toxic for public opinion in the Greek Cypriot community; in contrast, the provisions for a parliamentary system in the Annan Plan had been endorsed even by the strongest critics, including former president Tassos Papadopoulos.

The literature is fairly clear on the issue. Since the 1980s, Juan Linz has emphasised that 'presidentialism is less likely than parliamentarism to sustain stable democratic regimes' (Linz 1990; see also Mainwaring and Shugart 1997:449). Presidentialism tends to introduce a majoritarian ('winner-take-all') logic into democratic politics which is often incompatible with the very essence of power-sharing. Although the cross-voting amendments proposed in Cyprus might address some of these drawbacks, at least in theory, it is important to note that in the European Union there is currently no other comparable pure presidential democracy.

Turkey has recently moved towards presidentialism but remains an exception. In its report on the country's presidential referendum, the highly respected Venice Commission of the Council of Europe pointed to the multiple drawbacks of the presidential system. Interestingly, the report points out, "Turkey would become the only country with the presidential system and unicameral parliament in Europe, with the exception of Cyprus' (Venice Commission, 2017: 23). This unflattering comparison should be a source of worry for those mediators insisting on presidential choices in Cyprus and elsewhere across divided societies. The view that ethnically diverse societies are better served by parliamentarianism than by presidentialism is now widely accepted in comparative political science and is illustrated in contemporary failures of presidential regimes to secure democratic transitions in Egypt, Zimbabwe and Kyrgyzstan (McGarry 2013).

For these reasons, it is our belief that Cyprus should use the opportunity of a peace settlement to make a transition from presidentialism to a parliamentary system or a semi-presidential one at least. This could be inspired by this book's comparison of Brussels and Northern Ireland, but there are other models available, such as Switzerland, Canada or Belgium itself (see also Wolff, 2004). Such a transition could be supported by our analysis in the preceding pages and the various parliamentary and semi-presidential options suggested by our case selection. We suggest a wide range of alternatives: from the highly proportional system in Northern Ireland, to the disproportionality envisioned in Brussels, to the system requiring cross-party coalitions in Belgium, to one that relies on a simple automaticity in arranging the cabinet, as in Northern Ireland. While parties that exceed a particular threshold of seats in the Northern Ireland Assembly automatically qualify through d'Hondt for a certain proportion of seats in government, the system provides an additional democratic advantage in allowing each party to choose the particular portfolio in turn. This allows a party a strong opportunity to connect a seat in government to a key aspect of their political, economic or cultural interests.

The comparison of Brussels and Northern Ireland also suggests other differences relating to the manner in which consociations emerge; for instance, through cross-party mediations and referendum in Northern Ireland versus cross-party mediations and constitutional reform in the Brussels Capital Region.

More importantly, we argue that the particular political context is important and that divided societies like Cyprus should rely on their history and experience. For example, the 'presidential consociationalism' of the 1960 Zürich-London Agreements failed within three years due in part to a lack of internal consensus, though this would not have been the preferred institutional choice of consociational theorists in the first place, as we argued in Chapter 3 (Linz 1990; Lijphart 1994; McGarry 2011). Both historical and comparative evidence suggests the need for alternative models for Cyprus and there is certainly no reason for the island to continue on an institutional path that has already proven so problematic.

As we suggested in the preceding chapters, a Brussels-style or Northern Ireland d'Hondt system could provide a flexible starting point with the possible introduction of semi-presidential arrangements as an additional arbitration mechanism to resolve future deadlocks. Our proposed modification is relevant to cases beyond Cyprus, however. We believe it could also prove useful in Lebanon, Bosnia, Sri Lanka, Egypt and Colombia, to name only a few. Arguably, due to institutional path dependency, societies with presidential systems might be reluctant to move directly to a parliamentary system, making a semi-presidential compromise a safer first step. That said, we reiterate the need to avoid any conflicting powers between president and cabinet as well as the importance of paying attention to the overall details in designing and adopting new institutions in deeply divided societies.

Lessons for deeply divided societies and the Middle East

In our introduction to this book, we justify our case selection of Brussels, Northern Ireland and Cyprus in terms of their very different characteristics. These differences in geography, history and peace settlements give us the confidence to generalise our findings to other settings. The flexibility of the models presented herein allows for innovative thinking with broader relevance and wider applications.

Would the power-sharing arrangements described here be of interest to Syria or the broader Middle East? Although future studies should examine this question more closely, our findings suggest a significant potential for cross-learning. For one thing, the Brussels Capital Region offers a sensible and applicable model for the ethnically mixed cities of Syria, devastated by the civil war. The BCR region's two-tier system also offers a highly functional form of government integrating alternative schools of thoughts on power-sharing. For another, an all-inclusive executive such as the one in Northern Ireland might be easier to present and defend across the region because of its strong 'liberal consociational' elements than would other ethnic power-sharing alternatives, such as the Lebanese, Iraqi or Bosnian ones.[2]

In the simplest Northern Ireland form of inclusive government, membership in the inter-communal cabinet is automatically determined sequentially by electoral strength. If introduced in Syria, such a system would be inclusive of all political parties and also fairly functional, as parties would not waste time negotiating cabinet positions. By avoiding risky, polarizing and time-consuming negotiations following elections, the d'Hondt mechanism as described in this book generally eliminates potential dysfunctionalities and long delays in the formation of government coalitions. In Syria, this would broaden the participation of opposition groups, effectively encouraging power-sharing among the larger ethnic and religious groups without excluding other minorities, such as the militarily dominant Alewites or the potentially secessionist Kurds. If there is enhanced sense of buy-in from Kurds and others who may see advantages in participation, this would also have the advantage of reducing the potential for spoiler groups with little invested in the system to disrupt it. At the same time, it would avoid the tokenism common to the Iraqi and Bosnian models where 'ethnic representatives' might not necessarily represent the genuine interests of their group but may be appointed on the basis of their loyalty to a dominant leader or majority group.

The case of Northern Ireland is particularly informative and inspiring for conflicts in the Middle East. It suggests that power-sharing can be introduced in societies without any previous tradition of power-sharing arrangements, as, for example, Iraq or Syria. As noted in Chapter 1, Northern Ireland's earlier Sunningdale experiment with power-sharing was brief, lasting only a few months (1973–1974). But for those involved in the new experience of sharing power from the rival traditions of unionism and nationalism, d'Hondt proved to be a very effective means of stabilizing ethnonational relations – even in the absence of ceasefires and the continuation of political violence. It is important to note that d'Hondt-style models could also apply within groups to address competition between rival political parties in the Syrian and post-referendum Iraqi Kurdistan or in mediations involving Palestine's Fatah and Hamas currently progressing under Egyptian mediations.

Likewise, d'Hondt has been employed at the European Parliament in the allocation of the chairs of the parliamentary committees and could therefore be a useful mechanism for regional organizations such as the Arab League or the Organization of Islamic Cooperation, providing them the necessary toolkit to expand their capacity to support their member states.

How would it work in Syria?

We argue above that the Northern Ireland system of power-sharing has much to offer Syria. Moving beyond theory to practicality, how exactly could such a system be employed? Simply stated, the d'Hondt allocation provides a set of very simple formulas to estimate the number of ministries for each party and to draw the sequence with which parties choose ministerial positions (or any other positions at the central government or local levels). As noted earlier, d'Hondt requires simple divisions of each party's total votes (or seats) by one, two, three and so on. The party with most MPs (or votes) in each community chooses its preferred position in the government, and its quotient is divided by the appropriate divisor. If the same party still has the largest remainder, it chooses the second seat; otherwise it goes to the next largest party. The process continues until all qualifying parties have chosen all cabinet positions. Although we have discussed several examples from Belgium, Switzerland and elsewhere, the Northern Ireland model is the most formalised, quicker to form and suitable for low-trust environments, as in post-civil war Syria.

For one thing, Northern Ireland stands out across alternative power-sharing models in combining inclusivity and proportionality with automaticity in the formation of its Executive. By far, the main advantage of this mechanism for Syria and other highly polarised societies is the element of automaticity which implicitly reduces the veto powers of one community against the other and locks conflictual parties into a dependency for peace.

The system also allows smaller groups to either integrate with larger communities or vote for independent candidates, thus having an influence at various stages of the process. In the absence of reliable electoral data, Table C.1 presents a hypothetical scenario for Syria where future political parties would be entitled to seats in the Executive based on their level of representation in the assembly.

Such systems as demonstrated above create certain dynamics: when d'Hondt is used, the composition of the Executive is automatically determined based on electoral strength, not on negotiations between political parties following an election. Thus, all parties receive guarantees against future ostracism. Moreover, parties have an incentive to attract voters from other main or smaller groups to maximise their position in government; for

Table C.1 Hypothetical illustration of d'Hondt in Syria

Party	Party A (Sunni party)		Party B (Alewite party plus government allies)		Party C (e.g. Kurdish party)		Party D (e.g an intra-ethnic alliance)	
Divisor	S	M	S	M	S	M	S	M
1	34	1st choice	32	2nd choice	15	5th choice	9	
2	17	3rd choice	16	4th choice	7.5		4.5	
3	11.3	6th choice	10.6		5		3	
Total ministries	3		2		1		0	

S=seats in legislature; M=ministries. Parties vote divided by 1, 2, 3, . . . (d'Hondt divisor). Parties choose in order of highest quotient for six ministries. Order based on percentages here is A, B, A, B, C, A.

instance, Kurds would be enticed to attract Arab voters in their territories and vice versa. Finally, participation in a d'Hondt cabinet is entirely voluntary. If parties do not voluntarily assume their posts, others will be entitled to step in. Such inclusive methods respect all sides in a conflict and offer the simplest and fairest way to share power in deeply divided societies like Syria.

Conclusion: inclusivity as a lesser evil?

Our book provides a new conceptual understanding of intersecting theoretical areas of special relevance for peace and conflict research, including the framing of conflict management and transformation, the understanding of consociationalism and the renegotiation of power-sharing arrangements under unstable and changing conditions. We emphasise the micro-design of institutions and inclusivity as key principles in conflict management and transformation and argue that these principles could (and should) be transferred to other cases currently facing prohibitive conditions. We also demonstrate how to address prolonged deadlocks in forming governments through alternative deadlock resolution mechanisms, two-tier arrangements and the principle of automaticity. Our comparison of Brussels and Northern Ireland demonstrates a wide range of options in securing inclusivity. By way of contrast to our main cases, exclusive coalitions tend to increase uncertainty and competition among groups, as suggested in Lebanon, Iraq or Afghanistan, where groups have responded violently to attempts by others to ostracise them or minimise their influence. By extension, attempts to alienate one of the main ethnic or religious groups in Syria or elsewhere in divided societies across the globe might turn significant constituencies against the peace process. But a political system that invites parties to join the government on the basis of their democratic mandate will leap these hurdles and skip the most contentious aspect of consociationalism in divided societies – forming an inter-ethnic majority coalition.

Admittedly, no institutional solution can ever offer a panacea for all challenges facing post-conflict societies. By and large, institutional choices present difficult tradeoffs, in both the mediation and the implementation stages. While broad coalitions allow all major political parties to participate in democratic governance without exclusions, there is always a danger of radicals entering government. In addition, although the broader inclusivity ensured by engaging militants in democratic elections seems to work – as in Northern Ireland or more recently in Colombia – Western fears or ambiguity may delay positive learning across conflict zones. Perhaps the first and most important battle for new academic scholarship is to address those often-exaggerated fears and ambiguities.

What seems clear is that power-sharing can be adaptable to different contextual settings and to the specific conflict histories of deeply divided societies. It has proven to be adaptable and resilient, demonstrating a capacity to change over time in response to the political space available, as political parties and their electorates become accustomed to the institutions and their operation. This book argues that while consociationalism has been cast as merely a conflict management tool whereby deeply divided societies can learn to accommodate their differences, this underestimates its capacity to change over time. We have argued that power-sharing systems are capable of going beyond the parallel lines of political accommodation and distinct ethnonational behavior and that the protection provided to minority communities within such systems can promote the moderating dynamics promoted by advocates of centripetalist approaches. We have argued that it is time to get beyond the binary thinking evident within the consociationalism/centripetalist dichotomy and look at the possibilities for a hybrid model that takes advantage of both. *Mediating Power-Sharing* hopes to have made a contribution to that process.

Notes

1   Personal communication of second author with Derry/Londonderry municipal representatives, Derry/Londonderry, May 2011.
2   For instance, in Lebanon each key post in government is tied to a specific community group (e.g. according to the 1943 National Pact, the president is always a Maronite, the prime minister is a Sunni Muslim and the speaker of parliament is a Shia Muslim). Unlike Northern Ireland's liberal consociationalism, the Lebanese arrangement does not take into consideration proportionality and changes in the demographic composition of a country.

Bibliography

Council of Europe, CDL-AD(2017)005-e Turkey – Opinion on the amendments to the Constitution adopted by the Grand National Assembly on 21 January 2017 and to be submitted to a National Referendum on 16 April 2017, adopted by the Venice Commission at its 110th Plenary Session (Venice, 10–11 March 2017). www.venice.coe.int/webforms/documents/?pdf=CDL-AD(2017)005-e

Fernando Medina, L. & Loizides, N. (2013) Making Peace in Colombia: Is a Northern Irish Style Power-Sharing Possible? https://bacupblog.wordpress.com/2013/07/11/making-peace-in-colombia-is-a-northern-irish-style-power-sharing-possible/

Horowitz. D. (1985) *Ethnic groups in conflict*. Berkeley, University of California Press.

Horowitz, D. (2013) *Constitutional change and democracy in Indonesia*. Cambridge: Cambridge University Press.

Kerr, M. (2006) *Imposing Power-Sharing: Conflict and Coexistence in Northern Ireland and Lebanon*, Irish Academic Press.

Koneska, C. (2012) *Between Accommodation and Resistance: Political Elites in Post-Conflict Bosnia and Macedonia*, PhD Thesis, University of Oxford, St Antony's College.

Lijphart, A. (2004) 'Constitutional Design for Divided Societies.' *Journal of Democracy* 15 (2), 96–109.

Linz, J. J. (1990) The perils of presidentialism. Journal of democracy, 1(1), 51–69.

Mainwaring, S., and Shugart M. (1997) 'Juan Linz, Presidentialism, and democracy: a critical appraisal.' *Comparative Politics* (1997): 449–471.

McGarry, J., & O'Leary, B. (2007) 'Iraq's Constitution of 2005: Liberal Consociation as Political Prescription.' *International Journal of Constitutional Law* 5(4): 670–698.

McGarry, J. (2011) 'Centripetal Theory and the Cyprus Conflict', paper presented at the *Workshop on Power-Sharing*, organized by the Ethnicity and Democratic Governance Project, Munk Centre, University of Toronto, 17 November.

McGarry, J. (2013) 'Is Presidentialism Necessarily Non-collegial?' *Ethnopolitics* 12 (1): 93–97.

McGarry, J. (2017) 'Centripetalism, Consociationalism and Cyprus: The "Adoptability" Question.' *Political Studies* 65.2 (2017): 512–529.

McGarry, J., and Loizides N. (2015) 'Power-sharing in a re-united Cyprus: Centripetal coalitions vs. proportional sequential coalitions.' *International Journal of Constitutional Law* 13 (4): 847–872.

O'Leary, B., Grofman B. and Elklit J. (2005) 'Divisor Methods for Sequential Portfolio Allocation in Multi-Party Executive Bodies: Evidence from Northern Ireland and Denmark).' *American Journal of Political Science* 49 (1): 198–211.

Reilly, B. (2012) 'Institutional Designs for Diverse Democracies: Consociationalism, Centripetalism and Communalism Compared.' *European Political Science* 11 (2): 259–270.

Wolff, S. (2004) 'The institutional structure of regional consociations in Brussels, Northern Ireland, and South Tyrol.' *Nationalism and Ethnic Politics* 10 (3): 387–414.

Index

Note: Page numbers in *italic* indicate a figure and page numbers in **bold** indicate a table on the corresponding page.

For Product Safety Concerns and Information please contact our EU
representative GPSR@taylorandfrancis.com
Taylor & Francis Verlag GmbH, Kaufingerstraße 24, 80331 München, Germany

www.ingramcontent.com/pod-product-compliance
Ingram Content Group UK Ltd.
Pitfield, Milton Keynes, MK11 3LW, UK
UKHW021422080625
459435UK00011B/126

* 9 7 8 0 3 6 7 6 0 7 2 4 1 *